THE ETRUSCAN LANGUAGE
AN INTRODUCTION

FOR VITTORIA

GIULIANO BONFANTE

and

LARISSA BONFANTE

THE ETRUSCAN LANGUAGE

AN INTRODUCTION

NEW YORK UNIVERSITY PRESS
New York and London · 1983

First published 1983 in the U.S.A. by
New York University Press
Washington Square, New York, N.Y. 10003

Library of Congress Cataloging in Publication Data

Bonfante, Giuliano.
  The Etruscan language.
  Bibliography: p. 157
  Includes index.
  1. Etruscan language.   I. Bonfante, Larissa.
II. Title.
P1078.B58   1983   499'.94   83-13219
ISBN 0-8147-1047-6

Typeset in Monophoto Poliphilus by
August Filmsetting, Warrington, Cheshire

Printed in Great Britain

CONTENTS

ILLUSTRATIONS

PREFACE

The last twenty years have changed our view of the Etruscans. Excavations, discoveries, and new approaches have shown the history of this people in a way not before possible. Scholarly publications – catalogues, excavation reports, collections and monographs, beautifully illustrated and fully documented – are making available a wealth of material never previously usable for study. At the same time, the results of these new discoveries and research reach the interested public with remarkably little delay. The English translation of Massimo Pallottino's handbook, *The Etruscans*, edited by David Ridgway (1975), undid the barrier of language that often separates our students and a wider English-speaking audience from scholarly study of Etruscan history and culture. With Otto Brendel's *Etruscan Art* (1978), this translation opened a new period in Etruscan studies in English, a hundred years after the first publication of George Dennis' first-hand, still-classic account, *The Cities and Cemeteries of Etruria*. Historians, for instance in English Michael Grant, now for the first time write the history of the Etruscans independently of Rome.

The chapters on language in Pallottino's *Etruscans* set forth the evidence and warn of the hazards in the study of the Etruscan language. Pallottino's patiently repeated injunction that sterile discussions on the origin of the Etruscans, and the genetic connections of Etruscan with other languages, should give way to a consideration of the historical development of the culture and the language of these people, has finally won the day.

We attempt here to present the first concise but reasonably complete account of the Etruscan language in English. We hope to make our readers capable of consulting the works that collect and explain the material for the study of the Etruscan language: the *Corpus of Etruscan Inscriptions*, the *Thesaurus of the Etruscan Language*, Carlo de Simone's study of Greek

BACKGROUND

Map 1 Etruscan cities,
700–100 B.C.
(drawing by E. Woodsmall)

CHAPTER I

ARCHAEOLOGICAL
INTRODUCTION

Etruscan must be studied within a historical context. Like any other language, it was a creation of a particular people in a particular place, changing in the course of time. Then, too, Etruscan is known to us mainly through epigraphical documents, which need to be studied by linguists and archaeologists working closely together, since any interpretation of an inscription must take into account the provenance, date, and historical context of the monument on which it appears. A brief survey of the archaeological record is thus in order before we proceed to examine more closely the language known to us from these inscriptions.

Recent discoveries confirm the theory that the history of the Etruscan people extends from the Iron Age in Italy to the end of the Roman Republic – in chronological terms, from *c.* 1000 B.C. to *c.* 100 B.C.[1] Many sites of the chief Etruscan cities of historical times (map 1) were continuously occupied from the Iron Age 'Villanovan' period on. It has been pointed out that much confusion would have been avoided if archaeologists had used the name 'proto-Etruscan' instead of 'Villanovan' to refer to the Iron-Age material excavated near Bologna in the mid-nineteenth century, and later in all the major Etruscan sites.[2] For in fact the people who lived in central Italy between the Arno and Tiber rivers, whose language is first known from a thousand or so inscriptions of the seventh century B.C. (when we begin to refer to them as the historical Etruscans) did not appear suddenly. Nor did they suddenly start to speak Etruscan. What happened was that they learned to write from their Greek neighbours at Pithekoussai (Ischia) and Cumae,[3] thus revealing their peculiar language, and officially marking the beginning of the historical period in Italy.

Some archaeologists already recognize the ancestors of these historical Etruscans in the inhabitants of central Italy even before the Villanovan

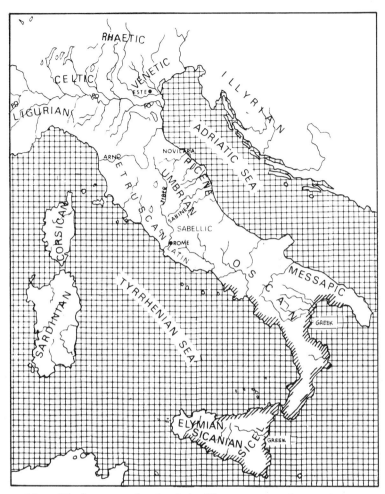

Map 2 The languages of ancient Italy, fifth century B.C. (G. Bonfante, P. Ferrero, *Grammatica Latina*, Milan 1976, map 2)

period.[4] Linguists have noted that the language we know is one which had already absorbed features of other languages from neighbours in Italy (map 2). Archaeologists and linguists agree, therefore, that the historical Etruscans had been developing their culture and language *in situ* – though they may disagree about the length of time – before we meet them in the epigraphic and historical record.

Two 'problems' which frequently come up in non-specialist discussions about the Etruscans, their language and their origins, need to be reformulated. In the first place, their language does not need to be 'deciphered', as the readers of this book know. In the second place, rather than the simplistic explanations of Etruscan origins still prevalent, based on Herodotus' story of a 'migration' from Lydia, or Dionysius of Halicarnassus' theory of an 'autochthonous' people of Italy,[5] we need a historical account of their formation and development. Etruscan origins are indeed well described in modern terms, in a recent history of the Etruscans, as the process of formation which culminated in early Etruscan history or protohistory: 'Perhaps the most important time in all its course was a period of a few decades that reached its climax in the eighth century B.C., for it was then that groups of adjacent villages – each group on its own defensible plateau – became amalgamated to constitute larger entities which before long became recognizable as the Etruscan cities and city-states.'[6]

This progressive urbanization of the Etruscan settlements explains how, by the end of the eighth century B.C., they were city-states ready to adopt the recent invention of writing, which spread with the same remarkable speed throughout Etruria as it had through Greece. As the more 'egalitarian' tomb provisions of the Villanovan period gave way to the princely elite furnishings of the seventh-century tombs of central Italy, at Tarquinia, Caere and Praeneste, the use of writing became the mark of a rich, sophisticated member of an aristocratic society. The alphabet, a purely Greek import,[7] was adopted as part of an Orientalizing style of life.

The earliest Greek inscription, a Homeric reference incised on the so-called Cup of Nestor (fig. 1), found at Pithekoussai,[8] within a few miles of Etruscan territory, shows that the Etruscans of the southern coastal cities had their Greek models ready at hand. It also points up the contrast between our knowledge of the Greek and the Etruscan language. The Etruscans adopted writing, and left behind them thousands of inscriptions, but no literature: They had no 'Homer, Sappho or Herodotus, with all that they mean for our contemporary Western culture: the memory of any conceivable spiritual adventure that accompanied the early flowering of Etruscan civilization was erased by its equally early decline. That is why the Etruscans and their remains are still remote, alien to ourselves and largely silent.'[9] Nor did they have the histories of Livy; as Momigliano points out, 'No necropolis, however rich, can ever replace the living tradition of a nation.'[10]

That the Etruscans had a rich religious literature we know from Roman tradition, confirmed by archaeological evidence (the Zagreb mummy) and linguistic evidence (glosses of plants and birds).[11] It is tempting to believe that their dramatic literature was also important;[12] but as often, the evidence is archaeological or visual rather than epigraphic or literary, giving us only elusive glimpses of such productions, incomplete and hard to interpret.

Νέστορος : ε[···]ι : εὔποτ[ον] : ποτέριο[ν]·

ℎὸς δ'ἀ‹ν› τόδε π[ίε]σι : ποτερί[ο] : , αὐτίκα κῆνον

ℎίμερ[ος] : ℎαιρ]έσει : καλλιστε[φά]νō : ᾿Αφροδίτες

'Nestor's cup was sweet to drink. But whoever drinks from this cup,
immediately the desire for Aphrodite of the beautiful crown will seize him.'

---

1 Nestor's cup, from Pithekoussai (Ischia). 725–700 B.C. (Photo
Soprintendenze Ant. Napoli e Caserta-Napoli). *Facing*: detail

The current tendency in Etruscan scholarship is to study their 'material culture' in its own time and try to understand the changes that came about in historical terms. So linguists, attempting to understand the structure of the Etruscan language and how it compares with that of other known languages, study Etruscan inscriptions in the context of the monuments on which they appear. In order to understand a monument's historical context, they need to know its date and provenance. The provenance, and the context, usually funerary, can often be established. The chronology cannot always be known from external evidence. Yet a monument can be classified at least as Archaic (seventh and sixth centuries B.C.) or later ('Classical' and Hellenistic, fifth to first centuries B.C.); and indeed this is the way most are identified in Pallottino's basic selection of Etruscan inscriptions, the *Testimonia Linguae Etruscae* (*TLE*, to which reference is regularly made). Linguists also distinguish two phases, archaic Etruscan and late Etruscan ('neo-Etruscan'). As the author of the grammar in this handbook points out, such a distinction is based on phonology, the first phase, seventh and sixth centuries B.C., being distinguished from the second (fifth to first centuries B.C.) by the gradual weakening of the vowels which takes place, in Etruscan, as in Latin, as a result of the intensive accent.

In order to provide a historical context for the provenance of inscriptions to be studied, it will be useful to survey the individual Etruscan cities, focusing on what archaeology has revealed about their writing.

The extent of the territory each city-state controlled varied in the course of time (map 1). Alliances between city-states, too, no doubt changed. Though tradition tells of the League of Twelve Peoples (i.e. Cities), and its centre at the Fanum Voltumnae, there is no indication that this League was anything but a religious federation.[13] Nor were these 'twelve peoples' the same in the course of time. We do know about the development of many of the important cities, however, mostly through their necropoleis.

Like the contemporary Greek cities, or the Tuscan cities of the Renaissance, these Etruscan cities were characterized by their individualism, independence and disunity. There never was an Etruscan empire. There was an Etruscan people, who shared a language, a religion, a geographical location, and certain customs and costumes which made them recognizably different from other people in Italy and in the Mediterranean. They also shared a name: the Etruscans called themselves Rasenna; the Greeks knew them as Tyrrhenians. This was the name given to the sea they controlled to the west of the Italian peninsula. The Romans called them Tusci. The name of one of the streets of Rome, the Vicus Tuscus near the

Capitoline Hill, long preserved the memory of their residence in the city.[14]

Beyond the differences from city to city, north and south were also generally distinguished by features of their art and language. The diversity of Etruria, rightly emphasized by Luisa Banti and other scholars since, must be kept constantly in mind. Those who have lived or travelled in Tuscany or elsewhere in Italy have experienced this diversity persisting in modern Italy, her glory and her weakness.

THE CITIES AND THEIR CEMETERIES

For our subject, it is important that each city specialized in a type of monument. Many of these were inscribed, as gifts to the dead or votive offerings to the gods; often, they contained epitaphs with name, family, age, rank, titles, and relationship of the deceased to the other members of the family.

The southern cities were the richest, especially the two coastal sites of Tarquinia and Caere.

Tarquinia

Tarquinia[15] (*Tarchuna* in Etruscan, *Tarquinii* in Latin) had the earliest flowering, in the Villanovan period; during the course of the Orientalizing period it was overtaken by Caere. Both cities were situated some distance from the sea, probably from fear of pirates. Tarquinia's port of Graviscae,[16] and Cerveteri's port of Pyrgi (map 1),[17] excavated within the last twenty years, have revealed sanctuaries and settlement areas and documented foreign relations in their inscriptions. The gold tablets from Pyrgi of *c.* 500 B.C. (fig. 5), written in Phoenician and in Etruscan, are very close to a 'bilingual' inscription, the Greek votive inscriptions from Graviscae reveal the existence of Greeks living in an enclave, on Etruscan soil, set apart from the Etruscan city. All these inscriptions have far-reaching implications for the Etruscans' relations in the Archaic period with Greeks and Carthaginians or Phoenicians, both those living on Etruscan soil and those of the mother country.

Tarquinia's pre-eminence and its status as an independent city-state were marked by its founding legend. According to this legend, Tarquinia was founded by and named after the hero, Tarchon, a figure whose story was closely bound with the traditions of all the Etruscan people. Tarchon,[18] the companion (or son, or brother) of Tyrrhenus, who led the Etruscans from Lydia to Italy,[19] was also the legendary founder of Pisa[20] and Mantua,[21] and was connected with the wise infant Tages, who invented the art of

haruspicina or divination, after being born from the earth in the fields of
Tarquinia.[22] According to other sources, Tarchon himself was the
inventor of divination from animal entrails,[23] and from the regions of the
sky, two techniques in which the Etruscans were particularly skilled.[24] A
mirror of the fourth century B.C. identifying Tarchon by means of an
inscribed label illustrates this event, and perhaps celebrates the foundation
myth, or 'history', of Tarquinia.[25]

One aspect of the story of Tages is of particular interest in connection
with the Etruscan language and alphabet, and the importance writing had
for the Etruscans, whose rites and religion were based on 'sacred books'.
The traditional account insists on the fact that Tages himself ordered his
revelation to be taken down in writing. A Praenestine cista, of the fourth
century B.C.,[26] unfortunately uninscribed, bears an engraved scene which
some have interpreted as Tages in the act of proclaiming his revelation,
which is being written down. In a book on prodigies a late author, John of
Lydos, even describes the writing in which Tarchon took down the words
of Tages in a 'different' kind of script, a statement some have taken to refer to
an earlier, pre-Etruscan syllabic script.[27]

Tarchon's – and Tarquinia's – story is thus related to important local
myths of the Etruscans: the legendary 'migration' of the Lydian group to
Italy, the foundation of cities in northern Italy, and the invention of
Etruscan techniques of divination. The city's great antiquity and prestige
among the Etruscans themselves is confirmed. The Romans, probably
rightly, thought of their own kings, the Tarquins, as coming from
Tarquinia, though later inscriptions record a *Tarchna* family from Caere.[28]

As at other Etruscan cities, it is the cemeteries that tell us of the life of their
inhabitants. At Tarquinia the characteristic chamber tombs carved from
the local *tufa* appear soon after 700 B.C. Covered with mounds, from the
mid-seventh century B.C. they were furnished more and more luxuriously.
Thousands of tombs have been explored since the beginning of the last
century. In the last twenty years alone six thousand have been identified by
the geophysical techniques of the Lerici Foundation.[29] The earliest
inscription known so far, on a Protocorinthian cup from Tarquinia, dates
around 700 B.C.[30]

Greek influence, always clear from the archaeological record of the tomb
furnishings, has been confirmed closer at hand than was thought with the
excavation of the Greek sanctuary at Graviscae. Once again, the traditional
account seems to fit the archaeological record. According to Roman
tradition a Greek aristocrat, Demaratus, having emigrated from Corinth as

a political refugee,[31] decided to settle in Tarquinia. There his son, Lucumo, or Lucius Tarquinius Priscus, later king at Rome, was born, grew up, and married. Demaratus is said by Pliny (*N.H.* 35.152) to have brought with him three terracotta sculptors, Eucheir, Eugrammus, and Diopus ('Skilled Hands', 'Skilled Draftsman', and 'User of the Level') – a remarkable testimony, in view of the importance of Greek, and especially Corinthian, influence on the art of Tarquinia (and other Etruscan cities), during the Orientalizing period, when Demaratus would have come. (His son, Tarquin, ruled at Rome traditionally from the end of the seventh century B.C., founding the dynasty which held the monarchy at Rome for one hundred years, until the beginning of the Republic 510/509 B.C.). Another early inhabitant of Tarquinia, whose grave and epitaph have been found, is Rutile Hipukrates:[32] like Demaratus, he lived in Tarquinia in the seventh century B.C. In the early second century B.C. Laris Pulenas describes his great-grandfather as *Creices*, 'the Greek'.[33]

From the mid-sixth century B.C. to the end of the Etruscan period, Tarquinia offers the largest continuous series of ancient paintings from the classical world decorating the walls of its tombs. The inscriptions included in these paintings consist of epitaphs, genealogies and labels. Though East Greek painters (refugees from the Ionian cities invaded by the Persians) evidently painted many of these, and started workshops staffed with Etruscan artists,[34] the style of the Archaic paintings and their subjects – aristocratic scenes of banquets, games, and luxurious living – reflect Etruscan taste and custom. They agree with Livy's description of Etruscan princesses attending splendid banquets 'in the company of their peers', in contrast to the chaste, virtuous Lucretia, who worked at her wool until late into the night surrounded instead by her maids.[35] The Archaic painting in the Tomb of the Bulls, one of the few with a mythological subject, shows Achilles' ambush of Priam's young son Troilus by the fountain outside Troy.[36] From a slightly later period come tomb paintings with gladiatorial fights – like the Romans, and unlike the Greeks, the Etruscans preferred spectator sports to athletic competitions, though these had been imported from Greece as well. One of these participants, wearing a mask, a pointed hat, and a special stage costume, is labelled *Phersu*.[37] Linguists agree in seeing here the origin of the Latin word *persona*, long used to mean 'character in a play', and only in recent times applied to 'personality' in the sense of a person's real identity. This word seems to fit the context of Rome's debt to the Etruscan theatre, which also brought into the Latin the Etruscan word *histrio* (cf. 'histrionics').[38]

In the fourth century B.C., a change comes in the subject matter of the tombs, which now represent scenes from the Underworld. One of the most impressive, the Tomb of Orcus, shows the souls of Greek heroes, for example *hinthial Teriasals*, 'the soul of Teiresias' (source 42; fig. 34)[39]. The divine couple of the lower world, Hades and Persephone, are also present. Mario Torelli has recently connected with the Spurinna family the painted representations of members of the aristocratic family whose epitaphs are proudly displayed in the Tomb of Orcus. Much later their *elogia* (statements of careers of generals inscribed on the bases of statues erected in their honour) were written at Tarquinia, in Latin, and now constitute a rare and precious historical document.[40] These *elogia* were written in the first century A.D., but incorporate material from family archives; they tell of honours received by citizens of Tarquinia in various military expeditions, probably in the fifth or fourth century B.C., against Syracuse, and it seems also against Caere and Arezzo.[41]

Another tomb, belonging to the Velcha family, is known as the Tomba degli Scudi, or Tomb of the Shields. Inscriptions inform us of its date and inhabitants. Here, as elsewhere, the generations of these aristocratic families are represented by couples, husband and wife together (a situation quite unlike the Greek, or Roman, idea of the male citizen, alone or in his public role).[42]

Apart from the tomb paintings, Tarquinia also produced stone sarcophagi bearing Etruscan inscriptions. Carved of *nenfro*, a local stone, of marble, or of alabaster, these stone sarcophagi are often decorated with figures or designs in relief on the front of the case, and represent the figure of the deceased reclining on the lid as on his banquet couch or death bed.[43] From the tomb of the Partunu family come several sarcophagi with interesting epitaphs, for example the one recording the career of Velthur Partunu, who died at the age of 82.[44]

The end of the Etruscan language at Tarquinia and the beginning of Latin is marked by the Latin inscriptions of wall paintings and of the grave markers or *cippi*, which came into use in the third century B.C., and of which we have about two hundred at present.[45] One tomb, the Tomba del Tifone, of the second or first century B.C., has wall paintings with funerary inscriptions in both Etruscan and Latin. Etruscan epitaphs commemorate the builder of the tomb, *Arnth Pumpu*, two of his sons, and a woman, *Hercna* (*CIE* 5412); while a Latin inscription identifies someone named *Tercenna*, probably belonging to the same family.[46] Here, as at Cerveteri, the language shift from Etruscan to Latin seems to have taken place around 100 B.C.[47]

Cerveteri

Situated around 45 kilometres from Rome, some 6 kilometres from the sea, Cerveteri, known to the Romans as Caere (Etruscan, *Cisra*; Greek, *Agylla*),[48] also had its Villanovan prehistory. Its period of greatest glory, however, was the Orientalizing seventh century, when it overtook and surpassed Tarquinia in importance and wealth. Its position on the coast, nearest to the southern boundary of the Etruscan area, put it in direct contact with the Greeks of Pithekoussai and overseas; and with the Phoenicians as well, as is shown by the bilingual inscriptions found in its port city, Pyrgi[49] (referred to as 'the towers' by the Greeks). The name of its other port city, 'Punicum', also recalls the Phoenician relationship.

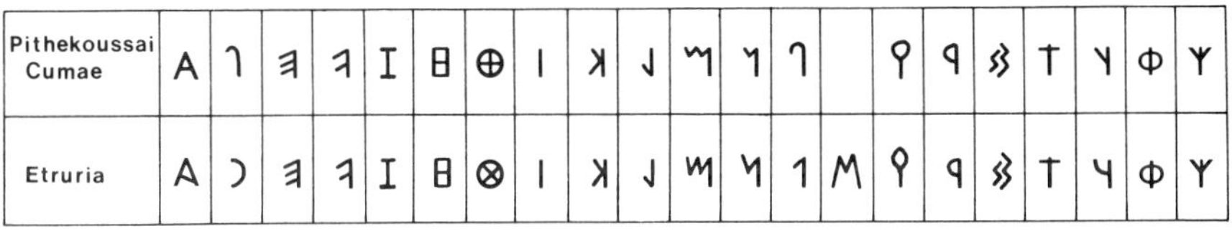

Pithekoussai Cumae	A	Ꮬ	�	Ꮩ	I	B	⊕	I	Ꮪ	Ꮷ	Ꮇ	Ꮁ	Ꮁ		Ϙ	�q	Ꮥ	T	Ꮍ	Φ	Ꭹ
Etruria	A	Ꭾ	Ꮙ	Ꮩ	I	B	⊗	I	Ꮪ	Ꮷ	M	Ꮍ	Ꮁ	M	Ϙ	�q	Ꮥ	T	Ꮍ	Φ	Ꭹ

2 The alphabet. Greek (Euboean) and Etruscan (Cristofani)

The Caeretans' trade in copper and iron from northern mines evidently allowed them to afford such luxury items as the massive gold, silver and bronze implements which they commissioned from local and foreign craftsmen. It may be that it was just for the purpose of such profitable trade that the alphabet was first adopted at Caere itself.[50]

It is important to note that the Orientalizing period so brilliantly exhibited in the chamber tombs of Cerveteri includes this importation and subsequent adoption of the alphabet, learned from Euboean Greeks stationed at Pithekoussai and Cumae, not far from Caere (fig. 2). Over thirty inscriptions from this period are known. The alphabet was adopted at a remarkably early date – perhaps even before 700 B.C. Here, as elsewhere, it was incised on writing implements which were placed in tombs as a sign of their owner's wealth and sophistication. One of these, a vase, perhaps a holder for ivory or bronze tools used to incise words on wax tablets, was included in the rich Regolini-Galassi tomb of the seventh century (source 2; fig. 12).[51] Made of bucchero, a black, shiny, metallic-looking ware which was a speciality of Caere's potters,[52] and six inches high, this vase was decorated not only with the usual alphabet, but also with a syllabary – letters in the form of syllables which were to be copied as an aid to learning the new art of writing. Other objects from the Regolini-Galassi tomb, now in the

Etruscan Museum at the Vatican, were engraved with the name *Larthia* (source 5; fig. 12).[53] The custom of inscribing the object with the owner's name, at Caere as elsewhere, before placing it in the tomb has provided us with many of the examples of Etruscan included in this book, in which the object states its ownership: 'I belong to Larth'.[54] Another seventh-century vase found at Tragliatella,[55] near Caere, was made by an Etruscan in imitation of a Corinthian vase. It bears a figured decoration which has not yet been satisfactorily explained, including a representation of armed soldiers in hoplite formation, erotic scenes, and a labyrinth-like shape, with the word *Truia*. Some have interpreted this as the name of the 'Trojan' game, the predecessor of the one which Augustus re-established at Rome.[56]

Caere, the most Hellenized of the Etruscan cities, was the only one to have a treasury at Delphi.[57] Her geographical position explains her extensive contacts with the Greeks. A Greek who signed himself Aristonothos painted a sea battle and the Homeric scene of the blinding of Polyphemus on a seventh-century vase found at Caere.[58] Greek artists came to Caere in the mid-sixth century and established workshops, producing special types of vases such as the 'Caeretan' hydriae with numerous mythological scenes.[59] It is intriguing to note that we know, from inscriptions, the Etruscan names of a number of vases, borrowed from the Greek.[60]

In the chamber tombs, which copy the designs of the houses of the living, rooms open out onto an entrance courtyard or *atrium* – the word, and the idea, may have come to the Romans from Etruscan architects.[61] The decoration is sculptured, rather than painted as at Tarquinia. Beds, chairs, shields are all carved out of the rock. A late tomb, the famous Tomba dei Rilievi, reproduces in relief all the furnishings of a home – pots and pans and pets, and, according to a recent theory, even a 'book' of linen, shown with its envelope, carefully folded on a chest.[62] Inscriptions were painted on the walls, as at Tarquinia: from these we learn that the tomb belonged to the Matuna family.[63] The inscriptions of the Tarchna family in another tomb may be of historical interest.[64]

The Caeretan style of writing, which has certain peculiarities, influenced the script adopted in the south, in Campania.[65] Caere's relation to the cities of Latium was also close: the great seventh-century B.C. Barberini and Bernardini tombs of Praeneste (modern Palestrina) best illustrate the influence of Caere.[66] In the Bernardini tomb, objects are inscribed for a woman, Vetusia; it is still not clear whether her name is Etruscan or Latin.[67] Other cities in Latium now being excavated also show in their art a close relationship with Caere in the seventh century and later.[68] Caere's relation with Rome, her neighbour, was one of close friendship. Some scholars have supposed that the Tarquins came from Caere.[69] Tarquinius Superbus and his sons, it is said, took refuge there after the dynasty was expelled from Rome at the end of the sixth century B.C. In the fourth century B.C. Roman nobles still sent their sons to Caere to complete their studies,[70] probably in technical subjects, especially the *etrusca disciplina* of the Etruscan *haruspices*, that is the art of divination and communication with the divine will that was prerequisite for a Roman general. Caere also served as the great Greek centre of the area, the 'Athens of the West'.[71]

Caere, the first Etruscan city to obtain Roman citizenship, eventually became Roman in language as in law, thus signifying the end of her independence. The monuments showing this transition from Etruscan to Latin are some three hundred grave markers or *cippi* from Caere.[72] These have texts sometimes in Etruscan, sometimes in Latin: there are even some bilingual inscriptions. As we would expect of epitaphs, all are quite brief. Because these cannot be attributed to individual tombs, from which they were removed often already in antiquity, they must be dated on epigraphic and linguistic grounds: 'The letter forms of the Latin *cippi* are those of the second or first centuries B.C.; and the archaic phonological features of Latin are almost entirely absent.'[73]

Veii

The wealth and power of Veii, the third great city of the South, started later than that of its two neighbours on the coast, but its inhabitants started to write as early as those of the other great Etruscan city-states. In the seventh century B.C., Veii adopted the alphabet, which we have in its 'model' form on a monument from nearby Formello (fig. 10).[74] In the sixth century, Veii became a great city-state, the most powerful in Etruria and second only to Rome in non-Greek Italy. Dionysius of Halicarnassus compared it to Athens (II.54). Five temples have so far been identified. One of these, of the mid-sixth century B.C., is among the earliest in all Etruria. Another, outside the city, in the sanctuary of Portonaccio − whose remains are still impressive today − dates from the last quarter of the sixth century.[75] Votive inscriptions found there suggest that the temple was sacred to Minerva (Menrva).[76] Its roof was decorated, in true Etruscan − but completely un-Greek − fashion, with free-standing, life-size terracotta figures representing Apollo (*Aplu*) struggling with Heracles (*Hercle*) over the possession of a hind, Hermes (*Turms*), and a goddess holding a child. Such representations of the gods in human form, which they adopted from the Greek world, the Etruscans passed on to the Romans, to whom they had a century before taught the Greek art of writing.[77]

Veii's ties with Rome were as close as Caere's, though of a different kind. Her artists' pre-eminence was recognized by the tradition that a terracotta sculptor from Veii, Vulca (the only Etruscan artist whose name has come down to us) was called in by Lucius Tarquinius Superbus (535–509 B.C.) to decorate the great Etruscan-style temple of Jupiter Optimus Maximus on the Capitol in Rome.[78] But Veii's proximity to the Tiber involved her in rivalry with Rome. Livy tells the story of this conflict with more detail than we have about any other aspect of Etruscan history. A ten-year siege culminated in the sack of Veii in 396 B.C. The destruction of the city marked the effective end of Etruscan power, overwhelmed by Rome to the south and the Gauls pressing down from the north. Sanctuaries at Veii evidently continued to function, but the absence of burial inscriptions, tombs or sarcophagi show that after the Roman conquest Veii was rarely inhabited.[79]

Five altars of the third century B.C. carry dedications to Roman gods in Latin. Three others carry dedicatory inscriptions dating from the same century, which bear the name, in Latin, or Faliscan, *L. Tolonio*, perhaps a member of the famous family of the legendary king of Veii, Lars Tolumnius. Veii seems to be the only city where the language shift from Etruscan to Latin took place before the end of the second century B.C.[80]

Vulci

Vulci, north of Tarquinia, 12 kilometres from the sea, was one of the first Etruscan sites to be discovered and excavated. The wealth it revealed had much to do with the popularity of the Etruscans in the nineteenth century, after the Prince of Canino, Lucien Bonaparte (Napoleon's brother), started 'mining' the cemeteries for gold jewelry, metalwork and pottery – he excavated huge quantities of Greek vases which today fill the museums of the world.[81] By 1842 the yield was said to equal that of Pompeii and Herculaneum; fifteen thousand tombs were opened by the middle of the century. Ironically, the sites are hardly published.

Already in the eighth century B.C. the existence of relations with the Greek centres of Pithekoussai and Cumae is clear from the style of vases. In the seventh century B.C. the wealthy tomb of the Polledrara necropolis (whose furnishings are today in the British Museum) testifies to Oriental and Greek influence and contacts in Vulci, as well as to its craftsmen's original taste and expertise in working bronze.[82]

In this century and the next huge quantities of Greek pottery were imported. The finds from Vulci contribute the largest absolute number of Greek vases available to us today – many more than those from Greece itself.[83] Greek wares were also imitated. Vulci was a great artistic centre, whose artists mastered a variety of crafts, including vase painting, stone sculpture, and – perhaps most famous of all – an important bronze industry. A bronze from Vulci was even found at Athens, on the Acropolis.[84]

Particularly interesting from our point of view is the Etruscan custom of incising inscriptions on the body of a statue – a custom which is found in Greece in the Archaic period, but which continues in Etruria, like many other Archaic features of art, social life and politics, long after it had been abandoned in the Greek centres. This custom was by no means limited to Vulci. The bronze Chimaera from Arezzo has on its leg the dedicatory inscription, *tinścvil* (source 22; fig. 19). A great many bronze statuettes bear, scratched into their carefully finished surfaces, letters recording the name of the person giving the gift, and the god to whom it has been dedicated. A number of these dedications include the word *fleres*, 'statue':[85] for example, a charming female statuette is thus dedicated to *Eileithyia* (*TLE* 734).[86] A bronze statuette of a *haruspex* in the Vatican says, 'this was dedicated by Vel Sveitus' (source 36; fig. 30).[87] A double-headed figure from Cortona was dedicated to Selvans, or Silvanus (fig. 30).[88] Even the life-size statue of the Arringatore, dating well within the Roman period, whose dress proclaims him to be a magistrate wearing the symbols of authority,[89] bears an inscription on the hem of his toga (fig. 37).[90]

Many objects for the tomb bear the inscription, *śuthina* (MVꓱINA in Etruscan script), that is, 'grave gift' (fig. 22). Sometimes it is brutally engraved on an object in such a way as to render it unusable. Mirrors, for example, sometimes have the inscription across the reflecting disc. This is a manner known also from other cultures of removing the object from the world of the living, dedicating it instead irrevocably for the use of the deceased.

Rarer than these dedicatory and funerary inscriptions, which may name the giver or receiver of the gift, is the artist's signature.[91]

Many engraved bronze mirrors,[92] an Etruscan speciality, were also surely made by the craftsmen of Vulci.[93] It is often not possible, however, to attribute these to specific cities because many have no record of their origin or tomb context. Yet these are the objects which more than any other give us information on Etruscan mythology, religion, and, on the linguistic level –

thanks to Eva Fiesel's pioneering study — on Etruscan phonology.[94]

From the fourth century B.C. dates one of the most important documents of early Etruscan history told from the Etruscan point of view. The 'François tomb' (source 43),[95] a chamber tomb whose rooms were decorated with a carefully planned and executed series of paintings, has inscriptions recording the triumph and augural status of the tomb's owner, as well as labelling characters from the legendary, local saga of the Vipinas (Vibenna) brothers and Macstrna. The latter, identified by the Romans as the king of Rome, Servius Tullius, is shown freeing a prisoner identified as Caile Vipinas; elsewhere Cneve Tarchunies Rumach (Gnaeus Tarquinius of Rome) is being murdered by an ally of Macstrna. The group is related in position, theme and political implications to another fresco opposite it with the Homeric scene of Achilles' slaughter of the Trojan prisoners (*Truials*) before the shade of Patroclus (fig. 35). The figures of the married couple, Vel Saties and Tanchvil Verati, the residents of the principal 'master bedroom' of the tomb, were also placed in relation with figures from Greek mythology. The whole decorative plan thus seems to make a specific statement, though it is not as clear to us today as it was to the designer of its iconography. The tomb in any case illustrates the anti-Roman feeling of the fourth century B.C., during the course of the violent wars between Rome and Vulci.

The Tomba delle Iscrizioni, containing archaeological material from the fourth century B.C. down to the first A.D., includes a number of inscriptions: seventeen in Etruscan and some six in Latin. The language shift at Vulci seems to have occurred in the first half of the first century B.C., in spite of the Latin milestone of the Via Aurelia (built in 241 B.C.), dating from 144 or 119 B.C.[96]

OTHER SOUTHERN CITIES

Other cities of southern Etruria are less important in the context of this book. Indeed the famous 'Tuscania dice', dating from the Hellenistic period, may not have come from Tuscania at all, but rather from Vulci.[97] Nevertheless it is true that at Tuscania, in the territory of Tarquinia, excavations of the last few years have brought many inscriptions to light. Archaeologically, Tuscania greatly resembles Tarquinia: the same type of *cippus* was used in both cities. At Tuscania, too, the use of chamber tombs continues uninterruptedly into the first century B.C.: the last of these tombs have Latin epitaphs.[98]

The alphabet incised on a delightful bucchero 'ink-well', now in the Metropolitan Museum of Art in New York (fig. 13), dating from the seventh century B.C., was apparently found in the region of the rock-cut tombs between Viterbo and Tarquinia.[99]

THE NORTHERN CITIES

The northern cities had access to the minerals so sought after by the Greeks. The exploitation of the metals of the area of Massa Marittima seems to have begun in the eighth century B.C., when the Greek markets of Pithekoussai and Cumae in Campania were founded in order to acquire them.[100] Not surprisingly, these northern cities were skilled at metal working, as well as copper mining.

Vetulonia

The earliest productions of Vetulonia (*Vetluna* or *Vatluna*) were wonderful sculptured figures of men and animals.[101] The gold work from the seventh century on was also very fine.[102]

There are other local specialities: the earliest examples of monumental Etruscan statues, male and female, come from the Pietrera tomb.[103] An inscribed grave stele of the late seventh century B.C. represents the fully armed warrior, Avele Feluske, holding an axe as the symbol of his rank and power (fig. 14).[104]

A study of Vetulonia's commerce shows that its contacts were rich and varied.[105] It traded with the north, with Chiusi and beyond (the area that provided the huge quantities of Baltic amber that figured in the tombs of rich ladies), with Sardinia, with the Greek cities, and perhaps with Rome, which seems to have derived the fasces from this northern city.[106] The bronze coins of Vetulonia, first issued in the third century B.C., bear letters identifying the city, and are decorated with anchors and dolphins – symbols which seem to indicate the importance of its overseas contacts.[107]

Within the territory of Vetulonia lies Marsiliana d'Albegna, from which comes one of the best preserved alphabets, on a miniature 'wax tablet', found together with other writing implements, styluses and ivory erasers (fig. 11).[108]

Populonia

Some forty kilometres up the coast from Vetulonia lies the dramatic site of Populonia: Etruscan *Pupluna* or *Fufluna*, 'the city of Bacchus', as we learn from a number of inscriptions, including the legends on its coins.[109] Indeed, Populonia may have been one of the first Etruscan cities to issue coinage, in the fifth century B.C. The Etruscans did without coinage far longer than the Greek cities. Many of their issues have the peculiarly Etruscan feature of bearing an archaistic design (though some scholars argue these are truly Archaic). The local coin designs include frontal Gorgon heads, and designs reminiscent of Populonia's interest in metallurgy.[110]

Volterra

Early material from the area of Volterra (Latin *Volaterrae*, Etruscan *Velathri*) includes the terracotta urn from Montescudaio, of the seventh century B.C., with one of the earliest representations of the theme of the banquet. Volterra was also from early times a bronze-working centre. Later finds include the grave stele of the warrior, Avile Tite (fig. 15).[111] Though not too different in type from the seventh-century grave-stone of Aule Feluske from Vetulonia (fig. 14), it dates from around 530 B.C.

Volterra's craftsmen specialized in sculpture. Most characteristic are the burial urns made to contain the ashes of the dead (cremation persisted in the northern cities). Many of these were inscribed, for example those of the Caecina (*Ceicna*) family, or clan, the leading family during much of Volterra's history.[112] Dating from the Hellenistic period, the urns constitute the single most important source for a study of the Romanization of the city. They are today much studied, from a variety of aspects: the typology of the 'portrait' figures reclining on the lids, the iconography of the mythological scenes carved on the front of the urn, the organization of the workshops which produced them.[113]

Fiesole

This city (Latin *Faesulae*, Etruscan *Vipsul*) stands today as the northern hilltop extension of Florence, the Roman city founded, as became customary, in the valley. Etruscan *Faesulae* was the northernmost city of Etruria, situated on a major route from the Arno north across a main Apennine pass.[114] It became a city only in the sixth or fifth century B.C. Most characteristic are the horseshoe-shaped gravestones with carved relief figures of the deceased and inscriptions listing their titles. These are related to the earlier Volterra stelae, and to those of Bologna (*Felsina*), which they influenced. Best known is the monument of Larth Ninie (fig. 17)[115] with spear and double-headed axe, similar to the Volterran stelai of Avile Tite (fig. 15)[116] and Larth Tharnie (fig. 16)[117]. There are few other inscriptions from this site.

Arezzo

This city, along with Fiesole, Perugia, Orvieto, and Cortona, was said to have been founded by the inhabitants of Chiusi (Clusium).[118]

Arezzo (Latin *Arretium*) some fifty kilometres away from Chiusi, stood on a plateau, between the northern extremity of the Chiana valley and the southbound curve of the Arno; unlike other Etruscan cities, on a gentle slope rather than a steep cliff. Strabo described it as the farthest inland of all the towns of Etruria.[119] Arezzo specialized in bronze work from early times. Its craftsmen made delightful small figures; and around 400 B.C. an artist created the famous Chimaera, the wounded monster, part lion, part snake, and part goat, with its dedicatory inscription to Tinia (Jupiter).[120] The Etruscans did superb work in bronze and skilfully imitated metalwork in terracotta. In the mid-first century B.C., Arezzo started to become famous in Italy and Europe for its shiny red, mold-decorated Arretine ware, with which it continued its earlier skill in metal working.[121] According to one theory, the fame of the northern Etruscan cities for their metal work led to the use of the word *Erz* to mean 'metals'. The Germans derived the term from 'Arezzo', which had come to mean metal *par excellence* (cf. Toledo blades, or China for porcelain, or Byblos for papyrus books).[122]

The fourth century B.C. was a difficult time for most of the cities of Italy, and Arezzo was no exception. There was a rebellion, perhaps a slave uprising. In 302 B.C. a Roman commander came to protect the wealthy, powerful, originally royal family of the Cilnii, ancestors of Maecenas, adviser and friend of Augustus. In the third century B.C. Arezzo passed peacefully into Rome's orbit.[123]

A 'peaceful process of Romanization' seems to be reflected in later inscriptions. There are three Etrusco-Latin bilinguals:[124] one of these can be dated to 40 B.C. on the basis of the grave contents; the other two seem to be later. Arretine pottery, too, specifically the *terra sigillata* with its stamped decoration, provides epigraphic evidence for the end of Etruscan: stamps were inscribed with letters, monograms, names or abbreviations, all in Latin.[125]

Cortona

This city was also a centre of bronze working, as shown by the famous decorated bronze lamp of the late fifth century B.C., now in its museum.[126]

Perugia and Todi

These two cities, in Umbria, became Etruscan and helped spread Etruscan culture into Umbria. The Etruscan alphabet was transmitted from Perugia (Latin *Perusia*) in the fourth century B.C., and used to write inscriptions preserving the local Umbrian language.[127] Both Todi (*Tuder*) and Perugia were also important for their bronze work; Perugia produced remarkable examples of bronze plates with *repoussé* decoration, as well as small bronze figures, while Todi contributed beautiful examples of bronze mirrors around 300 B.C. The remarkable, large-scale statue of the so-called Mars from Todi, of the early fourth century B.C., bears a dedicatory inscription in the Umbrian dialect (*Ahal Trutitis dunum dede,* 'Ahal Truttidius gave [this as a] gift'), though its style is clearly Etruscan.[128]

A famous epigraphic monument, the *cippus* from Perugia, probably a boundary stone, has a long Etruscan inscription running along both faces of the block, recording an agreement concerning two families, the Velthina and Afuna, in relation to certain lands and tombs. It dates from the second century B.C.[129]

Perugia offers rich tomb material of the late period, allowing its progressive Romanization to be observed more precisely than at other cities. Almost all the texts useful for such a study come from cinerary urns similar to those of Volterra and Chiusi. From Perugia come great family tombs, such as those of the *gens Rufia* (*CIE* 3649–3506), found intact in 1887, with five of the thirty-nine inscriptions in Latin; one of these is a bilingual. The tomb seems to have been in use from the third to the first century B.C.[130]

The tomb of the Volumnii (*CIE* 3763) includes one bilingual inscription on the marble urn of P. Volumnius Violens, of the end of the first century B.C.[131] It is exceptional in combining the Latin first name or *praenomen, Publius* with the family name or *cognomen, Violens,* designating an Etruscan. The tomb of the *gens Praesentia* records a person named *Presnte* and his mother in Etruscan, his wife and a third female in Latin. In the tomb of the *Pumpu Plute* family (*CIE* 3619–31), Etruscan inscriptions co-exist with Latin inscriptions. The Perusine War of 40 B.C. was a disaster for the city; it brought the end of the Etruscan tradition.

Volsinii

This may have been the site of the Fanum Voltumnae, the greatest Etruscan sanctuary and religious centre, whose exact location we do not know. (We do not hear of its existence, in fact, before the fifth century B.C.)[132] The site of Etruscan Volsinii (*Velsna*) is likewise unknown. Roman Volsinii was at Bolsena, and the French, who excavated a flourishing Etruscan city there, claim it as the site of the ancient Volsinii mentioned by our sources.[133] Other scholars think that Volsinii is to be identified with the important Etruscan site of Orvieto, whose Latin name (*Vrbs Vetus*) indicated its antiquity.[134] The territory of Volsinii included not only Orvieto and Bolsena, but took in Viterbo, at the edge of the area of Tarquinia, Bomarzo (Polimartium), Orte, Acquarossa and Ferentum, and others.[135] Lars Porsenna was also called king of Volsinii, perhaps because as king of Chiusi, he also ruled at Volsinii.

The city was evidently a great artistic centre. When Volsinii was destroyed by the Romans in 265 B.C., we are told, as many as 2000 statues were taken to Rome.[136]

In Roman Volsinii, cemeteries of the third, second and first centuries B.C. consisted of chamber tombs. Vases in the form of *askoi* have stamped on them the signature of one of the leading families of Volsinii, *Ruvfe*, Latin *Rufii*. Mushroom-shaped grave *cippi* bore the names of the deceased.[137]

Orvieto

Southwest of Perugia on a height overlooking the Chiana and Paglia Rivers, Orvieto (*Vrbs Vetus*, 'Old City') is one of the most important centres from the point of view of epigraphy. The Chiana Valley provided a direct link with Chiusi. Orvieto's heavy bucchero pottery is close to that of Chiusi, and the two cities use the same distinctive version of the Etruscan alphabet.[138] New excavations at the Crocefisso del Tufo cemetery promise to yield important material. The necropolis is one of the most beautiful in Etruria, giving the impression of an ancient Etruscan city with its regular streets, and neat doorways over which are written the names of the inhabitants, with the formula *mi suthi*, or *eca suthi*, 'I am the grave', or 'this is the grave'. In fact, the regularity and orderly consistency of these inscriptions, which appeared on each and every tomb, testify to an efficient civic organization, which passed and enforced zoning regulations on real estate property. Nothing like this situation in Archaic Orvieto is, for the moment, known elsewhere in Etruria.[139]

Chiusi

Chiusi (*Clusium* in Latin, *Clevsin, Camars* in Etruscan), dominating vast
and fertile valleys, depended for its wealth on agriculture. Its vast territory
included many smaller centres, which shared in its culture. Rich
necropoleis have yielded material from all periods, testifying to its stable
prosperity: much of this material was unfortunately dispersed and is hard to
date.[140] Recent study has shown that Chiusi, far from being isolated,
maintained important contacts with other Etruscan cities, with the world to
the north, to whom it brought such signs of civilization as writing and
wine-drinking, and with Rome to the south.[141] More than three thousand
inscriptions come from the territory, very few of them from scientific
excavation.[142]

The wealth of the *polis* can be seen from the quantity and quality of its
imports in the Orientalizing period, when gold, ivory, and Phoenician
bowls were brought in from the coastal cities. A Phoenician bowl of the
mid-seventh century bears the earliest Etruscan inscription from Chiusi, the
name of its owner, *Plikaśnas*.[143] Not long after, Chiusi was the chief centre
from which the Etruscan alphabet, and the use of writing in general, spread
northward to Bologna, Spina, the Veneto and the north-east Alpine
regions.[144] The northern type of alphabet in use in Chiusi became the
foundation of the Venetic and Rhaetian alphabets, and eventually of the
later Germanic runes.[145]

The sixth and fifth centuries B.C. saw a massive importation of Attic
black-figure and red-figure vases. The most elaborately decorated Attic
black-figure vase, the François vase, of the earlier sixth century, with its two
hundred or so mythological figures and careful labels in Greek, was found
near Chiusi. Recently restored and exhibited in the Florence Archaeological Museum, it may have arrived by way of Vulci.[146]

The territory of Clusium extended northward and apparently included
Murlo (Poggio Civitate),[147] whose ancient name is unknown. Recently
excavated, the site provides us with a precious example, along with
Acquarossa,[148] on the opposite edge of Chiusi's territory, of non-funerary
art and architecture. The discovery of tiles with letters of the alphabet incised
on them in the great building complex at Murlo provided Cristofani with
an opportunity to carry out a study of the alphabet of Chiusi and its
diffusion in centres directly influenced by the culture of Chiusi in the sixth
century B.C.[149]

Lars Porsenna, described as king of Etruria (an impossible title, though
indicative of the importance of his city), stands at the centre of a cluster of

heroic Roman tales of glorifying saviours of the city.[150] One in particular concerns Mucius Scaevola, who, mistaking the scribe who sat by the king for his intended victim, failed in his assassination attempt and proudly burnt his hand on the fire. The description of the scribe holding the tablets has recently been shown to fit into a peculiarly Etruscan artistic motif, represented visually on relief *cippi* from Chiusi of the Archaic period and later monuments, all of which show important figures, mortal or divine, holding scrolls or tablets. This motif of the book (cf. figs. 28 and 29), celebrating the importance of writing in Etruscan culture, is still present in the Hellenistic period, when male portraits of the deceased reclining on their sarcophagi have as their normal attributes a linen 'book' or scroll, or tablets.[151]

A tradition of close relations between Rome and Chiusi, at first sight unlikely considering the distance, may well be possible, in view of the excellent river and road communications with one another.[152]

In the Hellenistic period, the craftsmen of Chiusi turned to sculptured urns like those of Perugia and Volterra. On these, too, the inscriptions often survived. Easily recognizable by their style, these alabaster (or, more often, terracotta) urns had as favourite themes for their relief scenes the duel between Eteocles and Polyneices, and a battle scene, in which a god or hero by the name of Echetles wields a huge plough.[153] Other strange scenes and details show the continuing originality of Clusine artists and patrons.

It has been shown that the language shift from Etruscan to Latin took longer at Chiusi than elsewhere: many examples show that the progress of Latinization covered two or three generations. There are even married couples, and brothers, one of whom has an epitaph in Latin, another in Etruscan. Chiusi and Perugia together account for some ninety per cent of the inscriptions written in Latin characters which show Etruscan features.[154] In the linguistic area, as in its art, Chiusi shows itself to be conservative, to keep alive older features along with the new.

In conclusion, we see that the cities varied widely in their history and their art. Yet the use of the alphabet begins about the same time – early in the seventh century B.C. – in the south and north of Etruria, that is at the important cities of Caere, Veii and their neighbours in the south, and the great northern centre of Chiusi. The end of the Etruscan language is also contemporary, according to the research of Kaimio: 'The use of Latin epitaphs begins in the southern Etruscan cities probably at the end of the second century B.C., in north Etruria somewhat later. At this stage, many of the cities had acquired Roman citizenship.'[155]

By the later empire, Etruscan was a dead language. Aulus Gellius (*N.A.* 11.7.3f.) tells of a lawyer who used such archaic Latin words that his hearers laughed, as if they had been hearing Etruscan or Gallic. Evidently the story represents the Roman equivalent of our expression, 'it's Greek to me'.

NOTES

PART ONE

(Short titles refer to books listed in the *Bibliography*)

1. M. Pallottino, *The Etruscans* (1975) 42–57. For an excellent account of all these questions, with bibliography, see D. and F. R. S. Ridgway, *Italy Before the Romans*.

2. D. Ridgway, *CAH* (1980) 4, 12–13.

3. G. Colonna, 'Il sistema alfabetico', *L'etrusco arcaico* (Florence 1976) 9.

4. Ridgway, *CAH* 8.

5. For the history of the discussion, see L. Aigner Foresti, *L'origine degli etruschi* (Vienna 1974). D. Musti, *Tendenze nella storiografia romana e greca su Roma arcaica*. Quaderni Urbinati 10 (Rome 1970). Pallottino, *Etruscans*, Ch. 2. See also E. J. Bickerman, '*Origines Gentium*', *CP* 47 (1952) 65–81.

6. Grant 235.

7. Colonna, 'Il sistema alfabetico', 17–19, 51.

8. G. Buchner, C. F. Russo, 'La coppa di Nestore e un'iscrizione metrica da Pitecusa dell'VIII secolo a.C.', *Rendiconti Acc. Lincei* 10 (1955) 215–34. M. Guarducci, 'Nuove osservazioni sull'epigrafe della "coppa di Nestore"', *Rendiconti Acc. Lincei* 16 (1961) 3–7. E. Peruzzi, *Origini di Roma* II (Bologna 1973) 24–6.

9. Pallottino, *Etruscans* 238.

10. A. Momigliano, *JRS* 53 (1963) 98.

11. T. J. Cornell, 'Etruscan historiography', *Annali della Scuola Normale Superiore di Pisa* 6 (1976) 411–39. On the glosses, M. Torelli, *Mélanges Heurgon* 1001–1008. G. Bonfante, 'Problemi delle glosse etrusche', *Atti del X Convegno di Studi Etruschi e Italici. Grosseto 1975* (Florence 1977) 84. L. Bonfante, *Etruscan Dress*, 103–4, 153–4.

12. Heurgon 264–9. J. G. Szilágyi, '*Impletae modis saturae*', *Prospettiva* 24 (1981) 2–23.

13. Fanum Voltumnae: A. Pfiffig, *Religio Etrusca* (Graz 1975) 69–71; Pallottino, *Etruscans* 126, 129; Grant 211.

14. The name of the Etruscans: S. Ferri, *Studi Calderini e Paribeni* (Milan 1956) 111–15; G. Devoto, *StEtr* 28 (1960) 276; J. Heurgon, *MEFRA* 83 (1971) 9–28;

but see C. de Simone, *StEtr* 40 (1970) 153–81, L. Aigner Foresti, 'Tyrrhenoi und Etrusci', *Grazer Beiträge* 6 (1977) 1–25. *Vicus Tuscus*: Ogilvie, *Commentary, s.v.*; Pallottino, *Etruscans* 109. The Adriatic was so called from the settlement of Adria, or Atria, on the eastern coast, inhabited by Etruscans and Greeks.

15. Banti, *Etruscan Cities* 70–84; Grant 124–37. Boitani, *Etruscan Cities* 181–213; Torelli, *Etruria. Guida Archeologica*. M. Pallottino, *Tarquinia, Mon. Ant. Lincei* 36 (1937); H. Hencken, *Tarquinia. Villanovans and Early Etruscans* (Cambridge, Mass. 1968); M. Moretti, *Pittura etrusca in Tarquinia* (Milan 1974).

16. M. Torelli, *Parola del Passato* 26 (1971) 44 ff.

17. Pallottino, *Etruscans* 111–112. Grant 152.

18. Strabo, 5.219.

19. Herodotus, 1.94.

20. Cato, *fr.* 45 P.

21. Pallottino, *Etruscans* 97. Servius, *Aen.* 10.198, 200.

22. Johannes Lydus, *De ostent.* Praef. 3.

23. L. B. van der Meer, *BABesch* 54 (1979) 49–64. Pfiffig, *Religio Etrusca* 115–46. Dumézil 650–4.

24. According to Livy (1.34), Tanaquil read the omens of Tarquin's coming kingship in the sky; the Sibylline books of Rome were originally Etruscan (Ogilvie 46, 654–5, with refs.); and in the fourth century B.C. Roman youths were sent to Etruria to study, probably to perfect this art (Livy 9.36.3; Brendel 408).

25. Pfiffig, *Religio Etrusca* 45. M. Pallottino, 'Uno specchio di Tuscania e la leggenda etrusca di Tarchon', *Rendiconti Lincei* 6 (1930) 49–87; *idem*, 'Sullo specchio tuscanense con leggende di Tarchon', *StEtr* 10 (1936) 193.

26. F. Coarelli, *Roma medio repubblicana* (Rome 1973) 278–81, with previous bibliography. O. J. Brendel, *AJA* 64 (1960) 45 ff.

27. Johannes Lydus, *De ostent.* 2.6B. A. Hus, *Les étrusques et leur destin* (Paris 1980) 42, 175–7; cf. 163–4. But see E. Peruzzi, *Mycenaeans in Early Latium* (Rome 1980) 137–49. See Ch. V, n. 13.

28. M. Cristofani, *La tomba delle Iscrizioni a Cerveteri* (Florence 1965); *idem, CIE* II.1.4 (Florence 1970) 5907–74, *infra*, n. 69.

29. Pallottino, *Etruscans* 279–80.

30. Cristofani, 'Recent Advances', *IBR* 378.

31. A. Blakeway, 'Demaratus', *JRS* 25 (1935) 129–48. Ridgway, *CAH* 30–31. T. Gantz, 'The Tarquin Dynasty', *Historia* 24 (1975) 539–54.

32. Cristofani, *L'arte degli etruschi* 52. His first name, *Rutile*, is Latin (cf. Rutilius Namatianus), while *Hipukrates* is Greek.

33. Laris Pulenas: Pallottino, *Etruscans* 200, 219. Heurgon 292. For both of these see also Grant 126.

34. M. Cristofani, *Prospettiva* 7 (1976) 2–10; *idem, L'arte degli etruschi* 84–91.

35. Livy 1.57. Heurgon, *Daily Life* 86 ff.

36. Brendel 165–8.

37. S. Haynes, '*Ludiones Etruriae*', *Festschrift H. Keller* (Darmstadt 1963) 13–21.

38. Pallottino, *Etruscans* 180. A. Ernout, A. Meillet, *Dictionnaire étymologique de*

la langue latine (4th edn. Paris 1959–60) *s.v.*

39. Tomb of Orcus: Brendel 337–9.

40. M. Torelli, *Elogia Tarquiniensia* (Florence 1975), and review by T. J. Cornell, *JRS* (1978) 167–73.

41. Grant 135–6.

42. L. Bonfante, 'Etruscan couples and their aristocratic society', *Women's Studies* 8 (1981) 157–87. Cristofani, *L'arte degli etruschi* 136. Heurgon, *La vie quotidienne* 99–102.

43. R. Herbig, *Die jüngeretruskischen Steinsarcophage* (Berlin 1952).

44. Velthur Partunu, the so-called Magnate: Brendel 390.

45. Kaimio, 'The Ousting of Etruscan', 196–200. M. Pallottino, *Tarquinia, Mon. Ant. Lincei* 36 (1937) 377, 545–6, 559–60.

46. Tomba del Tifone: Cristofani, *L'arte degli etruschi* 200.

47. Kaimio 198.

48. Cerveteri (Caere): Boitani, *Etruscan Cities* 159–74; Banti 37–52; Grant 138–59, F. Canciani, F. ʻW. von Hase, *La Tomba Bernardini di Palestrina*. Latium Vetus II (Rome 1979). For the jewelry: G. Bordenache Battaglia, 'Gioielli antichi', *Il museo nazionale etrusco di Villa Giulia* (Rome 1980).

49. Pyrgi: *supra* n. 17.

50. For the wider diffusion of the alphabet and urbanization, see Cristofani, *Introduzione allo studio dell'etrusco* 8. Scholars have argued that the Greek alphabet was developed in order to record epic poetry, not just for economic needs: see A. Snodgrass, *Archaic Greece: The Age of Experiment* (London, Melbourne and Toronto 1980) 82, following H. T. Wade-Gery, *The Poet of the Iliad* (1952).

51. L. Pareti, *La tomba Regolini-Galassi* (Vatican 1947) 373, No. 413; Helbig, *Führer*[4] No. 653.

52. T. Rasmussen, *Bucchero Pottery from Southern Etruria* (Cambridge 1979). Cristofani, *L'arte degli etruschi* 54, fig. 2: map of Etruscan bucchero distribution in the Mediterranean, 630–550 B.C.

53. Helbig, *Führer*[4] Nos. 631, 637. Pareti, *Tomba Regolini-Galassi* 219, No. 152, pl. 16. The name is often taken to refer to a woman; but see M. Torelli, *DdA* 1 (1967) 39–40; F. Prayon, C. de Simone, *Aufnahme* 8. Source No. 5.

54. M. Cristofani, 'Il "dono" nell'Etruria arcaica', *Parola del Passato* 30 (1975) 132–52.

55. G. Q. Giglioli, *StEtr* 3 (1929) 111–59. Cristofani, *L'arte degli etruschi* 56.

56. Pallottino, *TLE* 74. A. Alföldi, *Early Rome and the Latins* (Ann Arbor 1965) 280–3, with preceding bibliography.

57. Cristofani, *L'arte degli etruschi* 98, 115. See also the gift of a throne by Arimnestos, 'who ruled among the Etruscans', in the sanctuary of Zeus at Olympia: Pausanias 5.12.3.

58. Cristofani, *L'arte degli etruschi* 45.

59. J. M. Hemelrijk, *De Caeretaanse Hydriae* (Amsterdam 1956); Brendel 171–4.

60. Colonna, 'Nomi etruschi di vasi', *ArchClass* 25–6 (1973–74) 132–50.

61. On *atrium* see A. Ernout, *Philologica* III (Paris 1965) 30. F. Prayon, *Frühetruskische Haus> und Grabarchitektur* (Heidelberg 1975) 159–60. Heurgon 188–92.

62. F. Roncalli, *JdI* 95 (1980) 263.

63. *Cippus* of Vel Matunas, in the Tomb of Reliefs, Cristofani, *StEtr* 34 (1966) 232.

64. *Supra* n. 28.

65. Colonna, 'Il sistema alfabetico', 22–3.

66. C. D. Curtis, *MAAR* 3 (1919); *idem MAAR* 5 (1925). Canciani>von Hase, *Tomba Bernardini* 5. Brendel 60–2.

67. Canciani>von Hase, *Tomba Bernardini* 39–40, No. 23. Principal dis> cussions: Heurgon 113. Alföldi, *Early Rome* 192; Torelli, 'L'iscrizione "latina" sulla coppa argentea della tomba Bernardini', *DdA* 1 (1967) 38–45. Cristofani, *Prospettiva* 5 (1976) 64, A. L. Prosdocimi, *StEtr* 47 (1979) 379 ff.

68. Colonna, in *Civiltà del Lazio Primitivo* (Rome 1976) 35.

69. *Supra* n. 28. Ogilvie 141.

70. Livy 9.36.3. Brendel 408.

71. Brendel 112.

72. Cristofani, *CIE* II.1.4, 'Caere'. L. Bonfante, review, *JRS* 66 (1976) 243–4.

73. Kaimio 194.

74. Formello alphabet: Pallottino, *Etruscans* 292, fig. 94. It comes from the same tomb as the Chigi vase in the Villa Giulia according to Colonna (*L'etrusco arcaico* 19). Veii's influence in Latium precedes that of Caere: Colonna, *Civiltà del Lazio Primitivo* 34–5; *idem, L'etrusco arcaico* 23. On Veii, see also Banti 52–62. Ridgway, *CAH* 9–16. G. Bartoloni, F. Delpino, *Veio* I (Rome 1979).

75. Brendel 237–45. Cristofani, *L'arte degli etruschi* 92–6.

76. Pfiffig, *Religio Etrusca* 58, 256–7.

77. E. H. Richardson, 'Etruscan Origin of Early Roman Sculpture', *MAAR* 21 (1953) 77–124.

78. Vulca: Livy 1.53.3. Pliny *HN* 35.157. O. W. von Vacano, *ANRW* I, 4 (1973) 528. Brendel 463, n. 27. M. Pallottino, *La scuola di Vulca* (Rome 1945).

79. Livy 1.5.33–50. Ogilvie 699–741. Banti 61.

80. Kaimio 205. Grant 220, 232. Lars Tolumnius, Livy 4.17; Ogilvie 558. L. TOLONIO DED. MENERVA: Pfiffig, *Religio Etrusca* 257. L. Vagnetti, *Il deposito votivo di Campetti a Veio* (Florence 1971), on *ex votos* offered to a female divinity protecting fertility; these last well into the first century B.C.

81. The account that follows is taken from G. Riccioni, 'Vulci: A topographical and cultural survey', in *IBR* 241–76.

82. *La civiltà arcaica di Vulci e la sua espansione. Atti del X Convegno di Studi Etruschi ed Italici* (Florence 1977). On the Polledrara Tomb, see also S. Haynes, *Ant.Kunst* 5 (1963) 3–4.

83. Beazley's indices of attributed vases include 1700 pieces from Vulci (Riccioni 269–271). Cristofani, *L'arte degli etruschi* 56–62. Seventy>five per cent of

all Attic pottery with known provenance from *c.* 525–500 B.C. comes from Etruria. A. W. Johnston, *Trademarks on Greek Vases* (Warminster 1979) 12. T. B. L. Webster, *Potter and Painter in Classical Athens* (London 1972) 157, 179, 227, 291.

84. Stone sculpture: A. Hus, *Recherches sur la statuaire en pierre archaïque* (Paris 1961). Bronzes: Riccioni 259–63 (bibliography and discussion).

85. On *flere(ś)* = 'statue' see A. Buffa, *StEtr* 7 (1933) 445–50. G. Sigwort, *Glotta* 8 (1916) 159–65. See also Gerhard, *Etruskische Spiegel* pl. 170. K. Olzscha, *Interpretation der Agramer Mumienbinde* (Leipzig 1939) 20–30.

86. Florence, Museo Archeologico 553. *TLE* 734. C. Laviosa, in *Arte e Civiltà degli Etruschi* (Turin 1967) 118, No. 328.

87. *TLE* 736. Bonfante, *Etruscan Dress* fig. 137.

88. Bronze male statuette, Cortona, Museo dell'Accademia Etrusca. Third to second century B.C. *TLE* 640. Pfiffig, *Religio Etrusca* 246–7.

89. T. Dohrn, *Der Arringatore* (Berlin 1968).

90. *TLE* 651. *CIE* 4196. Pallottino, with T. Dohrn, 'Nota sull' iscrizione dell'Arringatore,' *BdA* 49 (1964) 115–16.

91. Colonna, 'Firme arcaiche di artefici nell'Italia centrale', *RM* 82 (1975) 181–92. Craftsmen also used letters to guide them in assembling statues or complicated vases (Colonna, 'Il sistema alfabetico', 20).

92. The basic corpus is E. Gerhard, *Etruskische Spiegel*, completed by A. Klügman, G. Körte (Berlin 1840–97). J. D. Beazley, 'The world of the Etruscan mirror', *JHS* 69 (1949) 1–17, is a good summary in English. Recent interest in the subject has produced a large bibliography, including the first volumes of a projected *Corpus Speculorum Etruscorum*, organized by the Istituto di Studi Etruschi under Massimo Pallottino. D. Rebuffat-Emmanuel, *Le miroir étrusque* (Rome 1973) contains previous bibliography and discussion. See also Brendel, *passim*; *A Guide to Etruscan Mirrors*, ed. N. T. de Grummond (Tallahassee, Fla. 1982).

93. The school of Vulci has now been studied by U. Fischer-Graf, *Spiegelwerkstätten in Vulci* (Berlin 1980).

94. E. Fiesel, *Etruskisch* (Berlin 1931). C. de Simone, *Die griechischen Entlehnungen im Etruskischen* (Wiesbaden 1968–70).

95. F. Messerschmidt, A. von Gerkan, *Nekropolen von Vulci. JdI* 12, Ergänzungsheft (Berlin 1930). M. Cristofani, *DdA* 1 (1967) 186–219. Alföldi, *Early Rome* 220–231; *idem, Der frührömische Reiteradel* (2nd ed. 1979), 'Preface'. L. Bonfante, 'Historical Art, Etruscan and Early Roman', *AJAH* 3 (1978) [1980] 136–62, with previous bibliography.

96. Kaimio 204.

97. Pallottino, *Etruscans* 292, fig. 95. Colonna, 'I dadi "di Tuscania"', *StEtr* 46 (1978) 115. Other ivory dice: Helbig⁴ 2956 (from Praeneste, Barberini Coll.)

98. Kaimio 200. Banti 144–5.

99. Pallottino, *Etruscans* 115. Banti 108–9, 277–8, pl. 93.

100. Grant 178.

101. E. H. Richardson, *Archaic Etruscan Bronzes* (forthcoming).

102. Banti 134–5.

103. Hus, *Recherches* 100–34, pls. 1–3, 17–18. Bonfante, *Etruscan Dress* fig. 57. Brendel 92–3. Sprenger-Bartoloni pl. 47.

104. Pallottino, *Etruscans* 130, 280, pl. 30. Grant 83, 181, 183, 210, 268, 286. Scullard 223. Bonfante, *Out of Etruria* 37, 53, notes 26–34 (on the axe).

105. G. Camporeale, *La Tomba del Duce a Vetulonia* (Florence 1967); *idem, I commerci di Vetulonia* (Florence 1969).

106. Pallottino, *Etruscans* 129–30.

107. Grant 183.

108. Pallottino, *Etruscans* 291–2, pl. 93. Banti 116–17, 278–9, pl. 94. Peruzzi, *Origini di Roma* II 35–48. For the stylus used to write on these tablets, and other writing instruments, see J. G. Szilágyi, 'Un style étrusque en bronze', *Bulletin du Musée Hongrois des Beaux-Arts* 54 (1980) 13–27, with rich bibliography. Peruzzi, *Parola del Passato* 126 (1969) 181–3. Cristofani, in *Nuove letture di monumenti etruschi* (Florence 1971) 31–44, Nos. 16, 32, 38–9. Macnamara, *Everyday Life* 186. Cf. *infra* n. 151. For styluses from Marzabotto, see G. Gozzadini, *Di un' antica necropoli* (Bologna 1865) 33.

109. Grant 186–90. Pallottino, *Etruscans* 291, pl. 91. Banti 140.

110. Grant 189. L. Breglia, 'L'oro con la testa di leone', *Contributi introduttivi allo studio della monetazione etrusca. Atti del V Convegno del Centro Internazionale di Studi Numismatici, 1975* (Naples 1976) 75–85; discussion 131–9, 211–15. Breglia argues for a sixth-century B.C. date, against others who believe in a fourth- (or fifth-) century date. I am grateful to Tony Hackens for bringing this reference to my attention.

111. *TLE* 386. Pallottino, *Études Étrusco-Italiques* (Louvain 1963) 145, pl. 17.2. Bonfante, *Etruscan Dress* fig. 68. Brendel 133–4.

112. Grant 195, 201. Pallottino, *Etruscans* 136.

113. Basic corpus: H. Brunn, G. Körte, *I rilievi delle urne etrusche* (Rome, Berlin 1870–1916). Recent bibliography is enormous, starting from C. Laviosa's important *Scultura tardo-etrusca di Volterra* (Florence 1964). The *Corpus delle urne etrusche di età ellenistica* has begun to appear: Vol. I, *Urne volterrane. I complessi tombali* (Florence 1975), ed. by M. Cristofani. Most recently, with full bibliography: *Caratteri dell'ellenismo nelle urne etrusche. I Supplemento. Prospettiva* (Florence 1977), ed. M. Martelli, M. Cristofani.

114. Banti 161.

115. Banti 159. Bonfante, *Etruscan Dress* fig. 33. Cf. Cristofani, *L'arte degli etruschi* 140–141.

116. *TLE* 386. *Supra* n. 111.

117. From Pomarance, near Volterra. Florence, Museo Archeologico. *TLE* 407. Pallottino, in *Études Étrusco-Italiques* 148, fig. 18.1. Bonfante, *Etruscan Dress* fig. 69.

118. Grant 206–11. According to Livy (9.37.12), in 310 B.C. Perugia, Cortona, and Arezzo were among the most important cities of Etruria.

119. Strabo 5.2.9.226.

120. Brendel 327. *Infra*, source 22, fig. 19.

121. G. H. Chase, *Catalogue of Arretine Pottery, Boston. Museum of Fine Arts* (Boston and New York 1916). Revised by M. B. Comstock, C. Vermeule (Cambridge, Mass. 1975). R. M. Cook, *Greek Painted Pottery* (London 1960) 354–5, 374, esp. Ch. 7.

122. *Arezzo* and *Erz*: G. Bonfante, in *Out of Etruria* 127–30. Livy (28.45), listing the Etruscan cities who sent supplies for Scipio Africanus' campaign against Hannibal in 205 B.C., specifies the huge quantities of bronze arms and equipment contributed by Arezzo: Harris, in *Caratteri dell'ellenismo* 57.

123. Grant 208. Livy 10.3.2; 10.5.13. Harris, *Rome in Etruria and Umbria* 115, 201, 267, 320–1. Heurgon 318–28.

124. Kaimio 214–15. Bilinguals: *CIE* 378, 428; *TLE* 930. Pallottino, *StEtr* 23 (1954) 299.

125. *Supra* n. 121.

126. Pallottino, *Etruscans* 120.

127. *Ibid*, 119–120. Banti 176–8.

128. Vatican. Museo Etrusco Gregoriano. Brendel 317. T. Dohrn, in Helbig, *Führer*[4] No. 736. F. Roncalli, *Il 'Marte' di Todi* (Città del Vaticano 1973).

129. Pallottino, *Etruscans* 220, 292, pl. 98. *CIE* 4538. *TLE* 570.

130. Kaimio 210–13.

131. Pallottino, *Etruscans* 119, 278, pl. 22. A. von Gerkan, F. Messerschmidt, *Röm Mitt* 57 (1941) 122 ff.

132. *Supra* n. 13.

133. R. Bloch, *MEFRA* (1947) 99 ff. See Pallottino, *Etruscans* 115–16.

134. Grant 210–11. Banti 120: 'Up to 1946 the favorite hypothesis was the one identifying it with Orvieto. After the recent French excavations at Bolsena, many feel inclined to identify it with the Etruscan city above Bolsena'.

135. Pallottino, *Etruscans* 114–16. Grant 210–13.

136. Pliny *HN* 34.34. Banti 33. Brendel 293, 467, 470–1.

137. Kaimio 201–3.

138. Orvieto: Banti 121–7. Mario Bizzarri carried out excavations (*StEtr* 30 (1962) 1 ff.; 34 (1966) 3 ff.). Francesco Roncalli has resumed excavations. The most extraordinary discoveries come from the sanctuary of Cannicella, where the naked cult statue of a goddess was found: Pfiffig, *Religio Etrusca* 65–8.

139. Colonna, 'Il sistema alfabetico', 21–2.

140. R. Bianchi Bandinelli, *Clusium. Mon. Ant. Lincei* 30 (1925).

141. Cristofani, *L'arte degli etruschi* 136, and *passim*. L. Bonfante, *Out of Etruria*, Ch. 2, with bibliography.

142. Kaimio 206.

143. M. Cristofani Martelli, 'Documenti di arte orientalizzante da Chiusi', *StEtr* 41 (1973) 97–120. Sprenger-Bartoloni, No. 26, fig. 25.

144. Cristofani, 'Recent Advances', *IBR* 382; and 'L'alfabeto etrusco', in *Popoli e Civiltà dell'Italia antica* 6 (Rome 1978) 414–6, with fig. 6.

145. G. Bonfante, in *Out of Etruria*, 124–30, with bibliography.

146. M. Cristofani, *Il vaso François* (Florence 1981). Cook, *Greek Painted Pottery* 73–4, 318–19.

147. Cristofani, *L'arte degli etruschi* 131–8. *Poggio Civitate. Catalogo della Mostra* (Florence 1970). E. Nielsen, K.M. Phillips, Jr, *Notizie Scavi* 1976, 113–47, with bibliography.

148. C. Oestenberg, *Case etrusche di Acquarossa* (Rome 1975); Cristofani, *L'arte degli etruschi* 132–4.

149. M. Cristofani, K. M. Phillips, Jr. 'Poggio Civitate: Etruscan letters and chronological observations', *StEtr* 39 (1971) 409–30. Cristofani, 'Recent Advances', *IBR* 382.

150. Livy 2.9–15. Ogilvie 255, 270. Grant 217–8.

151. Livy 2.12.7. Colonna, '*Scriba cum rege sedens*', *Mélanges Heurgon* 187–95. Cf. F. Roncalli, *JdI* 95 (1980) 227–264, *supra* n. 108. For Mucius Scaevola, see L. Bonfante, *JRS* 60 (1970) 60, n. 71.

152. Grant 217–20.

153. Cristofani, *The Etruscans* 52. Brendel 380.

154. Kaimio 206–10.

155. *Ibid* 227.

THE LANGUAGE

CHAPTER II

INTRODUCTION TO THE LANGUAGE OF THE ETRUSCANS

Etruscans were already flourishing in Italy in the eighth century B.C., at the time of Greek colonization in the West, Phoenician trade, and the Orientalizing period of Greek art which spread throughout the Mediterranean. As noted in Chapter I, this period marked the beginning of the use of the alphabet in Greece and Italy. It is the alphabet, in fact, which reveals to us the people living in central Italy, between the Arno and Tiber Rivers, as Etruscans, writing in the Etruscan language. The problem of their origins, already discussed in antiquity,[1] is a linguistic one: their language is the only surely non-Indoeuropean language in Italy. There are a number of possible explanations for this fact, within the context of the complex movements of people in Europe and the Mediterranean in the protohistoric period.

Two things seem certain: there was no large-scale 'invasion', and they did not come during the historical period of Greek colonization. The language of the Etruscans reflects the influence of their neighbours, the Latins and the Umbrians (compare Latin *nepōs*, 'nephew', with Etruscan *nefts*), an influence which implies a certain period of proximity. Perhaps the arrival of a few Etruscans who came West during the 'international' period of the end of the second millennium is to be connected with movements of many groups travelling and settling in the Mediterranean during these complicated times of troubles. From the point of view of the Etruscan language the only real evidence of its Eastern connections – something more tangible than mere speculation – is the stele inscribed with a related language found on the island of Lemnos, dating from the sixth century B.C. (fig. 4). Here is a real contact with regions farther east; but we cannot yet base too much on a single find.[2]

The isolation and the originality of much of Etruscan custom fit in with

the alienation of a group surrounded by peoples speaking a totally different
language. For the ancient historians, the question of Etruscan origin was
also a problem. The Greeks had an answer available, since they were the
only ones to have a 'prehistory', the Homeric Trojan saga, with its many
heroes and their descendants. Thus a passage at the end of Hesiod's
Theogony, which may date anywhere from the eighth to the sixth century,
derives the Etruscans from the children of Odysseus and Circe.[3] More
complex is the case of Herodotus' report[4] concerning the Lydian origin of
the Etruscans. In Roman times, too, Vergil and Horace speak of Etruscans
as 'Lydians'. (Herodotus' source of information concerning Italy may have
been the western Greeks, who believed the barbarian Etruscans to be
descended from other barbarians, specifically the Lydians who were
neighbours of the Ionian Greeks in Asia Minor.) For Herodotus, the
origins of this rich people fitted another scheme of Greek history, that of
barbarian *truphē*, or luxurious living; for both Lydians and Etruscans had
the reputation, among Greeks, for luxurious habits and decadent morals.[5]

Dionysius of Halicarnassus, writing in 7 B.C., claimed that the
Etruscans were autochthonous. He too was influenced by a need to fit the
Etruscans into a scheme. The focus of his book, *Roman Antiquities*, on the
history of Rome and Italy, was to show that the Romans were not in fact
barbarians but originally Greeks. He proved this point by tracing Roman
origin to Greek sources, and by comparing Roman customs, institutions
and rituals whenever possible to Greek equivalents. In his view the Romans
were originally Greeks who had long ago immigrated into Italy. What,
then, was the status of the Etruscans, so clearly different in language and
custom? They must have been the 'natives': *they* were the barbarians, not the
Romans! In spite of his bias, Dionysius shows good ethnological method by
citing as evidence the languages and customs of the people involved.

And I do not believe either that the Tyrrhenians were a colony of the Lydians; for
they do not use the same language as the latter, nor can it be alleged that, though
they no longer speak a similar tongue, they still retain some other indications of their
mother country. For they neither worship the same gods as the Lydians nor make
use of similar laws or institutions, but in these very respects they differ more from the
Lydians than from the Pelasgians. Indeed, those probably come nearest to the truth
who declare that the nation migrated from nowhere else, but was native to the
country, since it is found to be a very ancient nation and to agree with no other either
in its language or in its manner of living.[6]

His statement that neither the Lydian language nor any other features of
their life show any similarity to the Etruscan has been confirmed by an

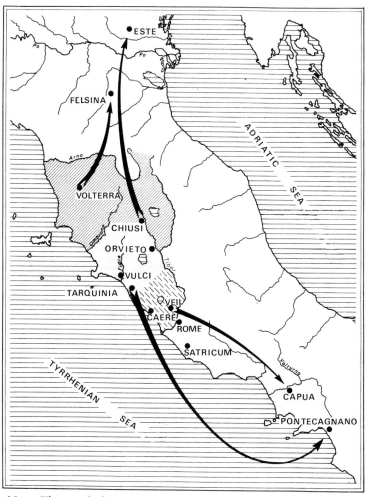

Map 3 The spread of the Etruscan alphabet in Italy (Cristofani, *Popoli e civiltà* 6, 1978, fig. 6)

analysis of the Lydian language, which is Indoeuropean, and therefore unrelated to Etruscan. Nor have excavations in Lydia turned up any particularly 'Etruscan' finds. Linguists worry about Etruscan origins today far more than archaeologists do. Archaeology shows clear continuity between the Etruscans of the seventh century and the prehistoric, Iron Age populations which preceded them in every major Etruscan city. Yet the Etruscans were a pocket of non-Indoeuropean speakers in an area where everyone else spoke an Indoeuropean language (map 2). Like the Basques, their language is different from that of any of their neighbours. Unlike the Basques, enclosed by high mountains and cut off from the rest of the world, the Etruscans controlled some of the richest, most fertile land in the Mediterranean, and its fine harbours along the coast. Obviously, the historical problem of the make-up of the Etruscan population is a complex one.

The Etruscan language can be traced through written documents from the seventh century B.C. to the first century after Christ. The Etruscans appear in Italy, within the international world of the Orientalizing period, as wealthy, spirited inhabitants of what later became Tuscany. From roughly 700 to 500 B.C. their power was at its height: they almost succeeded in uniting Italy from the Alps to Magna Graecia.[7] Their influence soon moved southward across the Tiber, taking over Rome itself, and all the cities throughout Latium, down to Campania, including Paestum (map 3). Rome and her neighbours thus received the full effect of the Etruscans' high civilization, all the outward signs of culture, the alphabet, the arts, the symbols and insignia of power. Greek culture first came to Rome by way of Etruria, for the Etruscans, having learned from the Greeks how to represent divinities in human form, build cities and temples, organize armies, drink wine, and use the alphabet, passed on many of these signs of civilization to their neighbours in Italy; and eventually, through the Romans, to all of Europe.

THE ALPHABET

Since a historical people is usually defined by its language, we speak of 'Etruscans' only from the day we have a text written in the Etruscan language, at the beginning of the seventh century B.C. We have, dating from this time, some inscriptions from Tarquinia, and some alphabets.

The invention of the alphabet, one of the greatest debts we owe the Phoenicians, changed the history of western civilization. According to the

Phoenician	Corinth	Athens	Ionia	Catchis and the West		Latin
ʾAleph	Δ	Δ	Δ	Δ	Alpha	A
Bet	ſ	B	B	B	Beta	B
Gimel	Γ	Λ	Γ	<, C	Gamma	C, G
Dalet	Δ	Δ	Δ	Δ, D	Delta	D
He	B	E	E	E	Epsilon	E
Vav	F	F	–	L, F	Digamma	F
Zayin	I	I	I	I	Zeta	Z
Het	B / –	B / –	– / B	B -h / – ē̄ } (H) Eta		H
Tet	⊗	⊗	⊗	⊗	Theta	
Yod	ξ	I	I	I	Iota	I
Kaph	K	K	K	K	Kappa	K
Lamed	Γ	ι	Γ	ι	Lambda	L
Mem	Λ	Λ	Η	Μ	Mu	M
Nun	N	N	N	N	Nu	N
Samekh	Ε	X	Ξ	⊞	Xi	X
ʿAyin	O	O	O	O	Omicron	O
Pe	Γ	Γ	Γ	Γ	Pi	P
Sade	Μ	–	–	Μ	San (=s)	
Qoph	Ϙ	(Ϙ)	(Ϙ)	Ϙ	Koppa	Q
Resh	P	P	P	R	Rho	R
Shin	–	ς	ς	ς	Sigma	S
Tav	T	T	T	T	Tau	T
	V	Y	V	Y	Upsilon	V, Y, U
	Φ	Φ	Φ	Φ	Phi	
	X	X	X	Ψ	Chi	
	✝	–	✝	–	Psi	
	–	–	Ω	–	Omega	

3 Table of alphabets. Archaic Greek and Latin

Roman historian Tacitus, the Phoenicians adopted the alphabet from the Egyptians. He also says that the Etruscans and the Latins – he calls them Aborigines – received their alphabet from the Greeks.[8]

We can follow the various phases of the alphabet, from the alphabetic Canaanite script of the Phoenicians, without vowels, to the Greek alphabet, whose innovation it was to adopt certain consonantal signs to signify vowels (A, E, H = Ē, I, O; and later, Ω, *omega*) (fig. 3). Because of historical conservation, we still recite the alphabet in the order in which the Greeks first received it.

From the Western Greeks originating in Euboea the Etruscans took over this invention which had been brought to Italy early in the eighth century B.C. (figs. 2, 6, 10). At first they copied the alphabet, just as they had learned it, as decoration on their vases and other objects. Very soon they adapted it to their own needs, dropping some letters that did not correspond to sounds in the Etruscan language and converting other letters to different uses.[9]

The Etruscan alphabet belongs, like the Latin, to the Western type of Greek alphabets, where *X* has the value of either a sibilant (*s*) or of occlusive *k* + sibilant *s* (*ks*). In Etruscan *X* = a sibilant (*ś*), whereas Latin *X* represents the occlusive *k* plus the dental sibilant *s* (*ks*, or *X*, as in English *axe*). (In the Eastern group of Greek alphabets, including Attic, *X* has the value of *ch*, as in Greek *chaos*, English *kin*, or *character*.)

On the other hand, the Etruscan alphabet also seems to preserve the traces of a very early Greek alphabet, older in part than the split between 'Western' and 'Eastern' Greek alphabets, since it preserves all three Phoenician sibilants, *samekh, sade* and *šin*, which neither 'Western' nor 'Eastern' Greek alphabet possesses any longer. (They have only one *s*, written with either *sigma* or *san*; archaic Etruscan had four, counting the sibilant *X*.)

The Etruscans evidently considered this alphabet to be decorative, and perhaps even magic, and copied it on various objects, especially vases, like those found at Viterbo, Caere, and Formello, near Veii (fig. 10). Most important is the alphabet from Marsiliana d'Albegna, dating from the seventh century B.C., inscribed on an ivory writing tablet originally decorated with gold leaf (fig. 11).[10] The one from Viterbo, now in the Metropolitan Museum, New York, decorates a bucchero container in the shape of a rooster which may once have held a coloured liquid like ink (fig. 8). These writing implements – we should add the bucchero vase or holder from the Regolini-Galassi tomb in Cerveteri – were placed in the tombs of rich people who were thus distinguished by displaying this new sign of civilization.

The alphabet thus displayed on the Marsiliana tablet and these other objects contains twenty-six signs, which can be transcribed as follows (below are the Latin equivalents; see figs. 2, 8, 10):

A B C D E F Z H Θ I K L M N S¹ O P S² Q R S³ T V S⁴ φ X
a b g d e v z h th i k l m n s¹ o p s² q r s³ t u s⁴ ph ch

Note: There are four symbols for *s*. Latin *v* is pronounced *w*.

The alphabet of twenty-six signs, given above, is called a 'model' alphabet. Some of the letters are never used as such (Italian school children also learn the signs *k, j, w, y*, which they never use in their own language). Of four signs for *s*, only two are used at any one time or place. Etruscan has no voiced stops – that is *b, g*, or *d* – and no *o* (see Chapter III). These signs are never used in early inscriptions, but they are included in the model alphabet, which reproduces the Greek model from which the Etruscan alphabet derives. This alphabet was adopted by way of Pithekoussai or Cumae, the Euboean Greek colony near Naples which was the home of the Sibyl described by Virgil, famous for her prophetic power. A Greek inscription of the eighth century B.C. on the so-called Nestor cup (fig. 1), recently discovered at Pithekoussai, confirms the hypothesis that the Etruscan alphabet came from that area.[11]

The direction of the writing usually goes from right to left, the reverse of classical Greek, Latin, or English, but the same direction as Phoenician and other Semitic languages, such as Hebrew. Lucretius may have had this peculiarity in mind when he talks of unrolling backwards the sacred verses of the Etruscans, hoping to discover the hidden will of the gods.[12] In archaic times *boustrophēdón* (also used in Greek) sometimes occurs, that is, 'as the ox ploughs', one line going from right to left, the next from left to right or the reverse. In more recent inscriptions of the third century B.C. or later we find that, under Latin influence, the direction goes from left to right. In this late period we even find some inscriptions in the Etruscan language written with a Latin alphabet, and some, in the Latin language, written with Etruscan letters.

In the earliest inscriptions the words are not separated at all, but the letters run on one after the other (*scriptio continua*). From the sixth century B.C. on, words are often separated from each other by a dot, or two or more dots placed vertically above each other (e.g. figs. 18, 21). Sometimes this 'punctuation' separates groups of letters within a word (fig. 20). Syllabic punctuation constitutes a peculiar feature of Etruscan writing (closed syllables are so marked.) Such syllabic punctuation is to be found on inscriptions of the mid-sixth to the end of the fifth century B.C. in southern Etruria and in Campania, but it ends about the time that the custom of separating words from each other has become the norm.[13]

Note on the transcription of Etruscan letters

Y = *ch* (*kh*) (aspirate: pronounced as in English *chaos* or *kin*)
ϴ O = *th* (aspirate: pronounced as in English *tin*)
Φ = *ph* (aspirate: pronounced as in English *pin*)
S, ⊞, X = *s* (pronounced as in English *sin*)
M = ś (perhaps pronounced as in English *shin*).
K = *k*, as in English *think*
Τ = *t*, as in English *stunt*
Λ = *p*, as in English *thump* or *split*

Note: For the pronunciation of Etruscan, the difference among the four *s*'s, and further remarks on the alphabet, see Chapter III. The Italian pronunciation of the vowels is used in this book.

THE EXTENT OF THE ETRUSCAN LANGUAGE

The first Etruscan texts can be dated around the year 700 B.C., though Etruscan must have been spoken in Etruria for quite some time before it was written. This is shown by a number of reciprocal influences and exchanges of words between Etruscan and the Latin and Italic[14] languages of their neighbours, as well as borrowings from their Geeek neighbours in Italy. The latest Etruscan inscriptions date from the time of Augustus (d. A.D. 14). By the time of Christ's birth, very little Etruscan, if any, was spoken. The mummy bandages in Zagreb, our longest Etruscan text (fig. 38), probably of the second-first century B.C., apparently contain several mistakes, which may indicate that the language was no longer really used.[15] It probably long continued to be read and used by priests as a sacred language, however, as Latin was in modern times. In A.D. 408, when the Gothic chieftain Alaric threatened to destroy Rome, Etruscan *fulguriātōres* visited the Roman emperor and offered to perform certain magic operations, reciting special formulas in order to avert the sack of the city by the barbarians. Clearly at that time the Etruscan religion and Etruscan priests still existed, as did their prayers and incantations, presumably in the

Etruscan language.

As to the geographical extent of the Etruscan language, inscriptions have been found mostly in Etruria proper, but also in Latium, Campania, northern Italy, Corsica and North Africa.

ETRUSCAN TEXTS

The total number of Etruscan inscriptions (incised on stone, lead, clay vases, and bronze mirrors, painted on the walls of tombs, etc.) is about 13,000. This is an enormous number, if we consider how few we have for the other non-Latin languages of ancient Italy. Eleven inscriptions describing a religious ritual, the Iguvine tables – written partly in an Etruscan, partly in a Latin alphabet – are all that remains to us in writing of the Umbrian language. There are a few hundred, altogether, of Venetic and Oscan. There are only three inscriptions of the language of the Gauls, and none of the indigenous idioms of Sardinia and Corsica. Of the Faliscan language there are more – some 150 inscriptions (this is probably due to the fact that Falerii belonged politically to Etruria). Of archaic Latin itself we have very few indeed. Before the third century B.C. (the date of the earliest epitaphs, the inscriptions of the Scipios, and of the beginning of the first literary texts, by Naevius, Ennius, and Plautus) there are only nine inscriptions, including one new one, and one shown recently to be a forgery. From the point of view of culture, Etruria appears in ancient Italy as a great centre, second only to the Greeks of South Italy. For a time, indeed, Etruria exercised on Rome the same kind of influence that was later exercised by the Greeks. We know from Livy (9.36.3) that in 310 B.C. the Romans still used to send their sons to study in the Etruscan city of Caere, just as they sent them later to Athens or Rhodes.[16]

Most of these 13,000 or so inscriptions (and more are constantly being discovered) can be understood. But the majority only contain the name, patronymic or father's name, sometimes the matronymic or mother's name, and the surname of the deceased. Sometimes there is also the age and the public office held; more rarely, if the deceased was a woman, the name of the husband and the number of children. The repetitions are innumerable.

What would be known of the English language if there were hardly anything but tombstones left to read? Very little. And of Etruscan there is even less. We do not even know the word for 'husband' (Etruria was not a matriarchy, so that we know only the name of the 'wife (*puia*) of so and so,' not, 'so and so's husband.'). We probably know the word for 'brother',

ruva; but not for 'sister'. Quite recently the word for 'father', *apa*, has been discovered;[17] yet this, too, is mentioned only a few times.
Only a few of the preserved texts are of any length.

1. The longest known Etruscan text is a sacred linen book, parts of which were preserved by being used as linen bandages on a mummy, found in Egypt by a Croatian traveller. The mummy was given to the Zagreb National Museum in Yugoslavia, where it is still preserved today. How this text came to Egypt in the first place is not known. Perhaps some Etruscan brought it there and then threw it away. A poor Egyptian, who could not afford to buy new bandages, might have used this cloth, after cutting it up into strips, to wrap up the mummy of his relative or friend, the woman who was found inside them. Even as it is, spotted and damaged by blood and the unguents used for mummifi-cation, it is uniquely precious (*TLE* 1).[18] (Source 54, fig. 38).

The text clearly represents some kind of sacred calendar, but unfortunately its detailed interpretation is largely doubtful. It contains prayers, names of gods, dates (the words 'day', 'month', and 'year' appear). There are at least twelve vertical columns, containing about 1200 readable words; but, as is often the case with religious texts and prayers, there are many repetitions. The actual number of new words this text brings is little more than 500.

2. The next-longest inscription is on a tile from Capua, of the fifth or fourth century B.C. Sixty-two lines are preserved, with almost 300 words that can be read (*TLE* 2).[19]

3. A text written on both sides of a lead plate, found in fragments near Santa Marinella on the sea, dates from around 500 B.C. Inscribed in a miniature style, it contains traces of at least eighty words, of which forty or so can be read with certainty (*TLE* 878).[20]

4. A small, lenticular-shaped, lead plate found at Magliano (probably dating from the fifth century B.C.) has a strange spiral inscription, running from the exterior margin inwards toward the centre. There are about seventy words (the division of words is not always clear) (*TLE* 359).[21]

All the above contain religious, ritual texts.

5. An important find took place at Pyrgi, the harbour of Caere, in 1964: three gold tablets, of which two are in Etruscan and one in Phoenician, recording the same event; a fourth text, in bronze and fragmentary, also had an Etruscan inscription. They date from around 500 B.C. The longest Etruscan inscription has sixteen lines and thirty-six or thirty-

seven words (*TLE* 873–877) (fig. 5; pp. 52–56).

6. Among the later inscriptions, on stone, is a *cippus* (probably a boundary stone) from Perugia: on two of its four faces is a sharply engraved inscription of forty-six lines and 130 words. The date is the second or first century B.C. (*TLE* 570).

7. The *elogium* or epitaph of Laris Pulenas of Tarquinia is engraved on a roll that the figure of the dead man holds in his hands as he reclines on his stone sarcophagus as if on a couch. It has nine lines and fifty-nine words, which can be in large part interpreted by means of a comparison with the Latin *elogia* (honorary epitaphs) of the Scipios, at Rome (*TLE* 131).

8. The famous bronze model of a sheep liver from Settima, near Piacenza,[22] is divided into many sections, each of which contains the names of one or more gods (there are fifty-one names, but several are mentioned twice or three times). The sections of the liver correspond to the sections of the sky which were under the protection of each of the gods. There was a mystic correlation between the parts of a sacred area, like the sky, and the surface of the liver of a ritually sacrificed animal. A teaching device, it was meant to be used by the Etruscan priest for his divinatory practice of reading the entrails of animals. According to the place where the liver of a sacrificed animal showed some special mark, the priest could guess the future, or even bend it to his will. The Etruscans were particularly skilled in this *haruspicina*, or science of reading omens, and the Romans respected, hired, and imitated them. A number of names of divinities appear not only on the liver, but also in a copy of an ancient text that Martianus Capella (fifth century A.D.) included in a Latin work, *The Marriage of Mercury and Philology*.[23] This work was enormously popular throughout the Middle Ages, thus preserving some of this esoteric lore into modern times. (*TLE* 719, fig. 36).

Shorter inscriptions, too, are of great importance. Painted inscriptions labelling figures in wall paintings in the tombs of Tarquinia and on engraved mirrors illustrating scenes drawn from Greek mythology make the interpretation of many words easier. The frescoes from the François Tomb at Vulci are particularly interesting, for they are historical, and celebrate victories over Rome (*TLE* 293–303). Other, shorter inscriptions occur on mirrors, painted vases, armour, furniture, coins, votive offerings, and a variety of monuments.[24]

A remarkable inscription from outside Etruria, written in an alphabet and a language akin to Etruscan, is a stele with the figure of a warrior, found in 1885 at Kaminia on the island of Lemnos and dated in the sixth century B.C. Its inscription has 198 letters, forming thirty-three words (fig. 4). The letters are divided from each other by two dots. Although the inscription cannot be called Etruscan, the writing and the language are similar. As in Etruscan, the alphabet used is derived from Western Greek, that is, Chalcidian, really Euboean, and there are no signs for *b, d,* or *g*. Words, endings, and even some expressions are strikingly similar to Etruscan. A formula indicating the age of the dead man, for example, *aviš sialchviš,* 'of forty years', is remarkably close to an Etruscan inscription which speaks of a man who died *avils machs šealchls,* '(when he was) five-and-forty years old'. (*TLE* 98). What this similarity to Etruscan means is still not clear.[25]

4 Stele from Lemnos. 6th century B.C. Athens, National Museum

CHAPTER III

THE STUDY OF THE ETRUSCAN LANGUAGE

Scholars have been able to make cautious but steady progress toward the understanding of the language by using a variety of methods, including the close study of bilingual inscriptions, of glosses, comparisons with other languages, archaeological context, internal evidence — all of these separately and in combination.[26]

BILINGUAL INSCRIPTIONS

We have some 30 Latin–Etruscan bilingual inscriptions. These are unfortunately not nearly as helpful for the understanding of Etruscan as the Rosetta Stone was for our understanding of Egyptian. Not only are they very short; they also contain free translations, rather than exact word-by-word equivalents.

The discovery at Pyrgi in 1964 of three gold tablets with inscriptions in Etruscan and Phoenician (fig. 5) was an outstanding event in the history of Etruscan studies, and allowed scholars to make some progress, though not great strides, in understanding the language of the Etruscans. Their greatest contribution was in the fields of religion and history. Found at the sanctuary of Pyrgi, the port of Caere (Cerveteri), the Etruscan city which most influenced Rome and served as mediator for Greek culture in Italy, they give tangible proof of the Phoenician presence in Italy at the end of the sixth century B.C. (just as the Greek sanctuary at Graviscae has emphasized the importance Greeks had in Etruria in the archaic period).

Of the three gold tablets, the one in Phoenician script and the longer of the two Etruscan ones can be said to be 'quasi-bilingual'. The fact that the ruler of Caere felt it necessary to publish a Phoenician translation of his religious dedication may attest to a close relationship with Carthage, or with

Cyprus, another important Phoenician centre at this time (*c.* 500 B.C.).[27]
The approximate dimensions of the tablets are 19 × 9 cm. The
Phoenician inscription consists of eleven lines and some thirty-nine words
(not counting prefixes or suffixes). The longer Etruscan inscription,
containing sixteen lines and thirty-six or thirty-seven words, is one of the
longest Etruscan inscriptions found to date. The shorter Etruscan
inscription has nine lines and fifteen words (*TLE* 874–5).

Both the longer texts record a historical event: the dedication of a cult
place and perhaps a statue to the Phoenician Astarte, or Ishtar, here
identified with the Etruscan Uni (and thus the Roman Juno), by Thefarie
Velianas, the ruler of Kyšry' (the Phoenician name for the city of Caere or
Cisra, now Cerveteri). This he did out of gratitude for a favour the goddess
had granted him – perhaps because she had raised him to power – in the
third year of his reign.

The Phoenician inscription is more specific about these events, recording
the exact months when they took place, and, for the favour received, the
exact day. The duration of the statue is counted as being as many years long
'as these stars'. There is a question as to whether this means 'years without
number', or whether it refers to some precise number of years.

The longer Etruscan inscription (*A*) describes, additionally, rites carried
out in reference to the events by which the goddess' favour had evidently
shown itself.

The shorter Etruscan inscription (*B*) refers to other ritual procedures
established by Thefarie Velianas to be carried out annually, or at the
anniversary of the foundation of the sanctuary.

Phoenician Inscription
LRBT L'ŠTRT 'ŠR QDŠ
'Z 'Š P'L W'Š YTN
TBRY'. WLNŠ MLK 'L
KYŠRY'. BYRH. ZBH
ŠMŠ BMTN' BBT WBM
TW. K'ŠTRT. 'RŠ. BDY
LMLKY ŠNT ŠLŠ III BY
RH KRR BYM QBR
'LM WŠNT LM'Š 'LM
BBTY ŠNT KM HKKBM
'L

5 Pyrgi tablets with Phoenician (Punic) and Etruscan inscriptions. c. 500 B.C.

¹To the Lady Astarte. This is the sacred place ²which has made and has given ³Thefarie Velianas (TBRY' WLNŠ), king over ⁴Cisra (KYŠRY'), in the month of Zebah ⁵(ŠMŠ) as a gift in the temple and ⁶in the enclosure (?); because Astarte has favoured her votary ⁷in his kingdom's year three [because Astarte wanted with her hand for me to rule for three years] in the ⁸month of KRR on the day of the burial of the ⁹deity. And the years of the statue of the divinity ¹⁰shall be as many years as these ¹¹stars. [may (they) be as many [as the stars of El (= god)]].

The Two Etruscan Inscriptions

(A)

ita. tmia. icac. he
ramasva [.] vatieche
unialastres. themia⟨
sa. mech. thuta. thefa⟨
riei. velianas. sal.
cluvenias. turu⟨
ce. munistas. thuvas
tameresca. ilacve.
tulerase. nac. ci. avi⟨
l. churvar. tesiameit
ale. ilacve. alsase
nac. atranes. zilac⟨
al. seleitala. acnasv⟨
ers. itanim. heram⟨
ve. avil. eniaca. pul⟨
umchva.

(B)

nac. thefarie. vel⟨
iiunas. thamuce
cleva. etanal.
masan. tiur
unias. selace.
vacal. tmial.
avilchval. amuc⟨
e. pulumchv⟨
a. snuiaph

(*A*) 'This is the temple (or chapel, cella) and this is the place of the statue (?) which he has dedicated to Uni⁄Astarte, the lord of the people (or king, or tyrant), Thefarie Velianas, *sal cluvenias* (?), he gave it, this one place (?); since on the one hand she raised him for three years (in the third year?) in this way, *churvar tesiameitale* (?) and since on the other hand he has been protected, here is the statue (or: in the month of August); (and may the) years (of the statue? be) as many as the *pulumchva*(?) (stars?)."

Notes

Thefarie in Etruscan = *TBR Y'* in Phoenician, cf. *Tiberius* in Latin, and the Etruscan name Thybris, etc., all related to the Tiber River[28] (Tiberius, found in Latin only much later, seems to have been a common Italic name much earlier than was thought).

ci avil = 3 years = ŠNT ŠLŠ III (three bars in the Phoenician text).

(*B*) ('Thus) here Thefarie Veliiunas established; the offering of the *etan* in the month of *masan* he offered; for the annual purification of the temple he made celestial (or: numerous or fruitful) *snuiaph* (ritual driving of the nails, or rites?).'

Notes

pulumchva – this word, appearing near the end of both inscriptions, has been connected with the Phoenician word for 'stars'.

avilchval – has the same root (*avil⁄*) as the word *avil*, meaning 'year'; here, therefore, translated as 'yearly', or 'anniversary'. *vacal tmial avilchval amuce*: 'the rite [libation] of the temple has been an annual one'?

If the Carthaginians were involved, Rome's 'paranoia' in regard to this hated rival can be better understood. The close political alliance between Carthage and the Etruscan ruler of Caere implied by these inscriptions would agree with Aristotle's statement about the constitution of Carthage and the Etruscans: Etruscans and Carthaginians were so close, he says, as to form almost one people.[29] The discovery of the inscription would also tend to corroborate the account that Carthage and Rome signed a treaty in 509 B.C., perhaps confirming an earlier one between Carthage and the Etruscan king of Rome. 'Rome of the Tarquins' re⁄emerges as an important, powerful city flourishing under Etruscan rule.[30]

Some thirty or so other bilingual inscriptions, in Latin and Etruscan, are in most cases funerary epitaphs of the second and first centuries B.C. Of lesser historical importance, they nevertheless provide important infor⁄

mation concerning Etruscan language and society and the relation between
the Etruscan cities and Rome near the end of the period of Etruscan
independence.

Here is an example (in all cases missing letters have been supplied and
abbreviations expanded):

Etruscan:	*cafates larth laris netśvis. trutnvt. frontac.*
Latin:	*L. Cafatius. L(uci) f(ilius) Ste(llatina tribu) haruspex fulguriator.*
Translation of the Latin:	'Lucius Cafatius, son of Lucius, of the Stellatina tribe, *haruspex*, interpreter of thunder bolts (*TLE* 697; stone, from Pesaro).

The problem here is that we have three words (*netśvis, trutnvt, frontac*) where
the Latin has two (*haruspex, fulguriator*). What is the translation of each of
the Latin words? Both *netśvis* and *trutnvt* occur at the end of two other
Etruscan funerary inscriptions after the name and patronymic of the dead
man, and therefore indicate his profession, some kind of priesthood. But
what of *frontac*? Apparently it goes with *trutnvt*: the Etruscans used a phrase
with two words to indicate a priesthood which in Latin had a single name,
fulguriator.[31]

Here is another bilingual:

Etruscan:	*cuinte. śinu. arntnal*
Latin:	*Quintus Sentius L(uci) f(ilius) Arria natus*

'Quintus Sentius, son of Lucius, son of Arria'. (*TLE* 523; on an urn from
Chianciano)
Cuinte is obviously the Etruscan transcription of *Quintus*; *śinu*, apparently, of
Sentius; since *arntnal* is the patronymic genitive, we have *natus*, or 'son' of
Arnt (or *Arnth*). *Arnt* apparently changed his name to Lucius when he
became a Roman citizen, and is thus referred to in the Latin version, which
is, surprisingly, the one which includes the matronymic *Arria natus*, a
typically Etruscan custom.

In another inscription the Etruscan has a matronymic, *Cahatial*, genitive
of the *Cahati* family name (*nomen gentile*) of the mother (-*i* is a feminine
ending in Etruscan). The Latin translation is *Cafatia natus*, or 'Son of
Cafatia'. The whole text reads:

Etruscan:	*pup(li). velimna au(le) cahatial*
Latin:	*P(ublius) Volumnius. A(uli) f(ilius) Violens Cafatia natus*
	'Publius Volumnius, son of Aulus, Violens, son of

Cafatia' (*TLE* 605; from Perugia, tomb of the Volumnii, in the Palazzone cemetery).

Pup(li) shows the Etruscan *p* for Latin *b*; *velimna* corresponds to *Volumnius, au(le)* to *Aulus*. When he became a Roman citizen, this *Publius Volumnius* added the Latin cognomen, *Violens*, to his Etruscan name. We are in the time of Augustus, in the last gasp of Etruscan civilization, as the decoration of the sarcophagus in the main tomb of the Volumnii clearly shows.

Another bilingual inscription, all in Latin letters, reads as follows:

Etruscan   *arnth spedo thocerual clan.*
                        'Arnth Spedo son of Thocero' (*K* 32, 47: 711–15).
Latin: *Vel Spedo Thoceronia natus*
                        'Vel Spedo son of Thoceronia' (cf. *Arria natus?*)

This marked the grave of two brothers, Arnth and Vel. (Their name, Spedo, shows Latin influence in the *d*.) We have here *clan = natus* (or *filius*). We already knew that *clan* meant 'son'. What is particularly interesting about this inscription is that the Latin is not a translation of the Etruscan. Each inscription is a separate epitaph for each of the two brothers: one brother, more conservative, records his name in Etruscan; the other uses Latin. This is the only Etruscan inscription where – certainly under Latin influences – the letters *d* and *o* are used. (The name Spedo very probably stands for Etruscan *Spitu*, known from other Etruscan inscriptions. *Spedo* is unknown in Latin.)[32]

Here is another bilingual, also on an urn from Perugia[33] (*TLE* 606; *CIE* 3692) on two lines, one Latin, one Etruscan:

Etruscan: *larth scarpe lautni* (on the body of the urn)
                        'Lars, freedman of Scarpus'
Latin: *L(ucius) Scarpus Scarpiae l(ibertus) Popa* (on the cover)
                        'Lucius Scarpus, freedman of Scarpia, priestly assistant'

Lautni means *libertus*, 'freedman', as in many other inscriptions. *Scarpe* has the usual nominative ending of Etruscan personal masculine names, '*-e*'. (Thus *marce* = Lat. *Marcus, plaute* = Lat. *Plautus, tite* = Lat. *Titus.*) The extra word in the Latin inscription, *popa*, is the title given to the priest's assistant who, at a sacrifice, killed the animal with an axe.

From the vicinity of Perugia comes a sixth bilingual inscription, also of recent times. It is probably not a coincidence that so many bilingual inscriptions were found at or near Perugia; this Umbrian city, though heavily influenced by the neighbouring Etruscan culture, was not originally Etruscan-speaking. The native language was Umbrian, and in fact we have Umbrian inscriptions from that area.

Etruscan: *larthi lautnitha presnts* (*CIE* 808; Cristofani 150).
Latin: *Larthi lautnita Praesentes*

Both inscriptions translate as 'Larthi, freedwoman of Praesens.' The Latin text was written by an Etruscan stonecutter, evidently the same person who wrote the first line in Etruscan, who knew little Latin. He writes *lautnita*, an Etruscan word, instead of *liberta*, and *Praesentes* instead of *Praesentis* (in the genitive case, 'of Praesens.').[34]

GLOSSES

Glosses, words translated into Latin or Greek and preserved for us by Roman or Greek authors, are also of use for our knowledge of Etruscan vocabulary. They have been collected and published by Massimo Pallottino.[35]

A number of the glosses that have come down to us preserve genuinely Etruscan words. Of Etruscan origin is the name of the entrance hall of the Roman house, the *ātrium*. *Aisar*, we are told by Roman authors, means 'god' in Etruscan (it actually seems to mean 'gods', in the plural); *uerse* (*uersum*) means 'fire'. *Aclus* is 'June'. Sometimes these translations can be checked from the inscriptions: the text of the Zagreb mummy wrappings, for example, has *aiser*, 'gods' and *acale*, 'June'.[36]

The great majority of glosses refer to words commonly used in the *etrusca disciplina*, the technique by which Etruscan *haruspices* read the will of the gods in the flight of birds, in lightning, thunder, or in the entrails of animals. Quite a few names of animals and plants seem to derive from some book on magic or medicinal herbs which was thought to be Etruscan.[37] Particularly interesting are the glosses informing us that the Etruscan word for 'monkey' is *árimos*. The word in Greek is *píthēkos*:[38] so *Pithekoûssai*, the ancient name for the island of Ischia, may have meant 'monkey island'. Another ancient name for *Pithekoûssai*, Lat. *Īnarimē*, may be the Etruscan name, also meaning 'monkey island'.[39]

Also important is the information that *lucumō* means 'king' in Etruscan. Lucius Tarquinius, who became king of Rome and founded the dynasty of the Tarquins, may have been originally called *lucumo*, or 'king'; his name may have been changed to Lucius when he became, so to speak, naturalized at Rome.[40]

A number of these words were not really Etruscan, but later seemed to Greek and Roman scholars to belong in the context of the Latin debt to Etruscan civilization, and were therefore thought to be of Etruscan origin. This is the case for words connected with music, like *subulō*, 'fluteplayer', or arms, like *balteus*, 'sword belt'. In fact, neither can be purely Etruscan, because of the *b*, which the Etruscans did not use. This material must obviously be used with caution. Other words identified as Etruscan in glosses, or 'explanations', by Greek authors, written in Greek letters, are also not Etruscan at all: *déa*, 'goddess', and *kápra* (Lat. *capra*), 'goat', are Latin words, not Etruscan, as their Greek glosses claim (*TLE* 851, 816, 828, 820). The letters *g*, *d*, and *b*, as we have seen, do not exist in Etruscan. The word *italós* is not Etruscan, although it has been claimed as such. *Italós*, that is *uitulus* (diminutive *uitellus*, from which derives the English word 'veal'), 'calf' in Latin, is the word from which the name of *Italy* (*Italia*) derives. It .was originally an Oscan word, which the Greek colonists of southern Italy adopted from the natives. Later Greek authors mistakenly attributed this word to the Etruscans in Italy, just as they attributed to them other words which came from Italy, but they knew were not Greek. The Greeks apparently did not distinguish clearly between the Etruscans and other peoples of Italy. When Rome was under Etruscan cultural influence and political domination, the Greeks must have thought of a Roman as an Etruscan. (In the same way we might say that some one is 'French' if he has a French passport, though he might be Basque, Flemish, Alsatian or Corsican by birth and language.)

Some glosses are clear, but not very useful. The statement that '*nepos* is an Etruscan word', which we find as a gloss, is quite correct. It confirms that the Latin word *nepōs* came into the Etruscan language, a fact we already knew from the inscription on the roll held on the sarcophagus of Laris Pulenas from Tarquinia, for example, where the word *nefts* appears.

A close study of Latin vocabulary reveals numerous debts to Etruscan. Most of these words occurred in the area of luxury and higher culture: the Etruscans introduced into Rome the words *persona* (from *Phersu*), *taberna, lacerna, laena, histrio*, as well as *atrium*. The very word for 'writing', *litterae* (from Greek *dipthera*, 'skin') came into Latin via Etruscan, just as the Greeks adopted the Semitic word *déltos* for their writing⁄tablets.[41] But all these words of Etruscan origin tell us more about early Rome's relations with her Etruscan neighbours than they do about the Etruscan language.

OTHER METHODS FOR THE STUDY OF ETRUSCAN

The so-called etymological method, which involves a comparison of Etruscan with other languages, living or dead, was widely used until about 1875, but gave little or no results. Though now completely abandoned by serious scholars, it continues to flourish in amateur circles. There is hardly any language in the world which has not at some time been compared to Etruscan: Greek, Armenian, Turkish, Aztec, Hittite, and many others. The 'mystery' of Etruscan, like that of the Great Pyramids, holds a fatal fascination for crackpots convinced that they can decipher the language, crack the code and find the key. Aside from that of the inscription from Lemnos, there is no other known language to which Etruscan can be compared. There are a number of Greek words in Etruscan, and there were certainly exchanges, in historical as well as prehistoric times, between the neighbouring Latin, Etruscan, and Italic languages, especially in the field of personal names. For example, the Etruscans learned to drink wine in Italy, and they learned what was by then the local word for it, *uinum*.[42] But these contacts have nothing to do with the basic nature of the language or its origin.

A number of scholars have used the technique of 'combinatory' analysis. This internal, inductive method, which was in part a reaction to the failure of the etymological method, resulted in considerable progress in the study of Etruscan grammar and of the translation of some inscriptions. Just as codes to which we do not have the key can be deciphered by trying out different combinations of letters until the right one is found, so in Etruscan different words are tried out in different contexts. Obviously the meaning of a particular word must make sense in the other contexts in which it appears and make a proper 'combination'. This method has been useful, but it is too limited to be used by itself.

Another approach is the 'quasi bilingual' method. The cultures of Italy were in close contact and similar in many ways. It is therefore reasonable to expect that a number of formulas were used in most of these languages (just as the English expression 'took place' has an equivalent in French *eut lieu*, or Italian *ebbe luogo*). Rituals described on the mummy bandages in Zagreb are, for example, comparable to those of another text, that of the Umbrian Iguvine Tables, from Gubbio (Lat. *Iguuium*) in Umbria. The funerary epitaph or praise on the roll of the Tarquinia sarcophagus of the 'Magistrate', Laris Pulenas, recalls the Latin epitaphs of members of the noble Roman family of the Scipios, likewise inscribed on their stone sarcophagi.[43]

The 'cultural' approach interprets words in the context of the object on which the inscription is found. A tomb, for example, will give us the names and titles of the people buried there, while a vase will be inscribed with the owner's name or the name of the god to whom it is dedicated or offered.

There are also what might be called picture bilinguals. Engraved bronze mirrors, vase paintings, and tomb paintings from Tarquinia have inscriptions which label or explain the various figures in the scene being illustrated. A number of these appear in the present book.

CHAPTER IV

THE PRONUNCIATION OF
ETRUSCAN

All alphabets when they are first used are strictly phonetic (though not always phonemic). Etruscan spelling retained this feature.[44] It never developed a 'historical' spelling, as used in English (where e.g. the *oo* of *spoon*, once pronounced with a long *o*, now has the same sound as the *u* in *rule*). In Etruscan an *a* (as in *father*) is therefore always pronounced *ah*, *i* (as in *machine*) is always *ee*, and so forth (with the Italian values). Changes in pronunciation, during the approximately seven centuries when Etruscan was spoken and written, were regularly reflected in the spelling (so when *ai* became *ei*, and eventually *e*, it was spelled the way it was pronounced: *Aivas > Eivas > Evas*.)

The Etruscans copied the Greek alphabet, exactly as they had learned it, in the so-called 'model' alphabets (figs. 2–3, 6, 10; Marsiliana d'Albegna *c.* 650 B.C.: Source 1, figs. 10a, 11) which they used for decorative or perhaps magic purposes. But for practical purposes they dropped those Greek letters they did not use: *d*, *b*, and *o*. For the sound *k* (English *think*) they used three signs: *k* before *a* (*ka*); *c* before *e* and *i* (*ce*, *ci*); and *q* before *u* (*qu*). Such a distinction (which is exclusively phonetic, that is articulatory, but has no semantic or 'phonemic' value) exists in German (cf. German *Katze, Kehle, Kuh*). The same system was used in early Latin. In English the three letters survive (*kernel, cat, quit*), all of them with the value of *k*. (In English there is no difference in function, as there was in Etruscan, between *ka*, *ce*, and *qu*.)[45]

Since they could not pronounce voiced stops, the Etruscans used the third letter of the Greek alphabet (*gamma*: Γ or *C*) with the value of *k* (see above). Imitating the Etruscans, the Latins did the same (see Latin *cēna, corium, cūra, catēna, cīuis*, all of them pronounced by the Latins with the value of *k* in English *think*). The *k* of early Latin survived before *a* in a few words (*Kaeso, Karus, Kalendae*).[46]

Model alphabet	Archaic seventh–fifth century B.C.	Neo–Etruscan fifth–first century B.C.	Pronunciation and transcription
			a
			k
			e
			w (v)
			ts
			h
			th
			i
			k
			l
			m
			n
			s
			p
			sh (s)
			k
			r
			s
			t
			u
			s
			ph
			kh (ch)
			f

ETRUSCAN NUMERALS

I	I (1)
Λ	V (5)
X	X (10)
↑	L (50)
C ✱	C (100)
⊙	C (100) or M (1,000)?
⊕	M (1,000) or M̄ (10,000)?

6 Table of Etruscan alphabets and Etruscan numerals (*Thesaurus* 421–2)

The third Greek letter, Γ (written *C*), in Latin was pronounced the Etruscan way, like a *k* (English *c* in *cat*), since the Latins had received it with this value. Further proof of the influence of Etruscan on the Latin alphabet is the use of *q* in *quālis, quattuor, queritur, quīdam, quoque*, and so on. For the sound *g*, which the Latins also pronounced,[47] they introduced, around 250 B.C., a new letter, *G* (which was merely a slight modification of *C*, adding a little mark to it). In order not to change the order of the alphabet, this new letter *G* took the place of the ancient *Z*, which at that time the Latins no longer used (it had formerly had the value of English *z* as in *zeal, zoomorphic*, etc.). Later, in the first century B.C., more intimate contact with the Greeks brought with it the need for *Z* in order to write Greek words. The Latins then reinstated this letter *Z*, which, having lost its place in line, was put at the end, where it still is today.

Both the Etruscans and the Latins eventually simplified the system of the velars. Arezzo in the north kept only *k*, while the southern cities kept only *c*. In Latin, *c* was generally used (under Etruscan influence), except before the semivowel *u* (as in *qualis*). The letters *c* and *q* are still used this way in English (*candy, quiz*).

The letter *z* in Etruscan always had a voiceless sound, as in English *gets, cats* (not as in *zeal*).

The Etruscan *v* was certainly bilabial, like Latin *u* in *uincit* (English *w*), since diphthongs like *au* are frequently spelled *av*: so *lautni: lavtni; avle: aule*.[48]

Since the Etruscans only had the voiceless stops *k, t*, and *p*, they changed the letters *g, d*, and *b* whenever these appeared in foreign words – Greek, Latin or Umbrian – to *k, t*, and *p*. (These they pronounced like the final consonants in the English words *think, spit*, and *thump*.) Thus from the Greek word *amórgē* came the Latin word *amurca*, 'oil dregs', by way of Etruscan. The Etruscans also wrote (and no doubt said) *creice* for *Graecus* (*TLE* 131). Etruscan also had the aspirate voiceless stops *χ, θ*, and *φ*, which in this book will be transcribed (as the Latins did) *ch, th*, and *ph*. These aspirate consonants were pronounced something like initial *k, t*, and *p* in *kin, tin*, and *pin*. (The difference between voiceless and aspirate consonants is one which the speaker of English hardly perceives, since it is a distinction which has, in English, no semantic or phonemic value, as it had in Etruscan – and has today, for example, in Chinese.)

There were several ways of representing sibilants, though not all were used at the same time in the same area. Four appear on the 'model alphabet' of the seventh century (fig. 10): the three-stroke *sigma* ⩤ ; *samech* ⊞ ; the *sade* Ⲙ (as in the archaic alphabet of Corinth); and a special cross sign

✕ . In the Archaic period in the north two signs were used, the three-stroke *sigma* Ƨ and the *sade* ᛗ . In the southern cities, such as Veii and Caere, and in Campania, the four-stroke *sigma* Ƨ was used as a variant of the three-stroke *sigma* Ƨ ; in the area of Caere, around the end of the sixth century B.C., this sign was used to represent a phoneme in opposition to the three-bar *sigma* Ƨ , representing another phoneme. In the southern cities of Veii, Caere, and Tarquinia the cross sign ✕ also took the place of the three-bar *sigma* in the Archaic period (from the end of the seventh to the mid-sixth century B.C.). And at Caere, in the later period, a new sign, something like a *3*, was developed from the Greek four-stroke *sigma* Ƨ .

We do not know for certain how these various *s*-signs were pronounced. They seem to have represented only two different sounds, since the Etruscans usually used only two different signs concurrently at any one time. Scholars conventionally distinguish two signs in transcribing Etruscan inscriptions: *s* and *ś*, perhaps pronounced as in *sin* and *shin*, respectively. ᛗ is transcribed as *ś*. They are indicated thus in Pallottino's basic collection, the *Testimonia Linguae Etruscae* (*TLE*), to which reference is given in the examples which follow.[49]

The Etruscans had a sound *f* (approximately as in English *find, soft, stuff*) for which the Greeks had no sign. At first the Etruscans wrote the digraph *FH* (*tavhe, vhelmus*, cf. *TLE* 56, 429, etc.) Later they adopted a new sign, *8*, the origin of which is obscure (it may be a modification of ⊟, which was used in initial position with the value of *H*, or *h*). The Latins, conversely, kept only the first element of the digraph, *F*, the letter familiar to us today with the sound of *f*.

The voiceless stops *k, t, p* sometimes alternate with *ch, th, ph*, for no apparent reason (*sec = sech*). But after the liquids *l, r, m, n*, we find only *ch*: *sulchva, fulumchva, flerchva*.[50]

f frequently alternates with *h* (as in Faliscan): *fasti: hasti*; *cafatial: cahatial*; *fastntru: hastntru*. This alternation of *h* with *f* may be due to Italic influence. *p* alternates with *f* (*pupluns: fufluns*).

After vowels the sounds *ch* and *c* are evidently interchangeable, since we have both *sech* and *sec, zilach* and *zilc, zach* and *zac, zich* and *zic*. But as verb endings the two sounds, *c* (or *k*) and *ch* definitely have different meanings, since *-ce* is the past active ending, as in *turce*, 'he gave', and *-che* is the passive ending, as in *mi menache*, 'I was given' (see below, Ch. IV).[51] Sometimes the two aspirates *th* and *ch* are also interchangeable: we have *zilath* and *zilach*.[52]

The Etruscan vowel system is simple. There are only four vowels, *a, e, i, u*.

The vowel *o* is absent; there is no reason to believe it ever existed. In the transcription of Latin and Greek words into Etruscan, the vowel *o* (and in Greek ω or *omega*) is always written as *u*: the Greek word *Phoînix* becomes *Phuinis*; *Achérōn* becomes *Achrum*; *Promētheús* becomes *Prumathe*. (As noted before, the rare cases of *o* to be found in Etruscan inscriptions, all of late date, are due to the influence of the Latin language.) The ancients themselves noted this absence of the letter *o*. The Roman author Pliny tells us that 'some peoples of Italy have no letter *o*, and use the letter *u* instead, specifically the Etruscans and the Umbrians'.[53] (Until they adopted the Latin alphabet the Umbrians, close neighbours of the Etruscans, shared this peculiarity, which for them was purely graphic, since Umbrian had the sound *o*.) The Etruscan letter *e* was pronounced like English *paint* or *bait*. It was a very closed vowel, as proved by the fact that it is often interchanged with *i*: so we see both *ica* and *eca, mini* and *mine, cliniiaras* and *clenar*, etc. The Greek name *Iason* (English Jason) becomes *Eason*; and the Etruscan genitive form *-ial* often becomes *-eal*. Etruscan had only short vowels (like several other languages, e.g. Spanish, Rumanian).[54]

Greek diphthongs are usually preserved, except that of course *oi* becomes *ui*. In later inscriptions (fifth to first century B.C.) *ai* often becomes *ei* (by assimilation of the first vowel of the dipthong to the second) and even *e*: so the Greek name *Aívas* (Ajax) is written as *Aivas, Eivas*, or *Evas* in Etruscan. *Graikós*, 'Greek', written *Graecus* in Latin, becomes *Creice* in Etruscan, and the name of the hero Aeneas, *Aineías* in Greek, is written *Eine* in Etruscan. We find this change from *ai* to *ei* taking place also in other Etruscan words, for example *aiser*, which becomes *eiser* in some late inscriptions.

There is a general trend toward the simplication of two different vowels, forming a diphthong, into a single vowel. The Greek sound *eu* is sometimes preserved (as in the name of the Muse *Euterpe*, who is called *Euturpa* in Etruscan), but *eu* sometimes becomes *u* in Etruscan, as for example in the name of Castor's brother Pollux, called *Polydeúkēs* in Greek, whose name in Etruscan becomes *Pultuce*. Latin *au* also becomes *a* in a number of Etruscan words.[55]

Sometimes extra vowels are inserted in consonant clusters in order to make words easier to pronounce. This tendency accounts for the transformation of the Greek name of the goddess *Ártemis* into *Aritimi* in Etruscan, or the Etruscan name of Hercules, *Hercle*, into *Herecele*.

Then, too, liquid consonants – both the nasals *n, m* and the vibrants *l, r* – are frequently 'vocalic'. The consonant is pronounced as though it were a vowel and could stand on its own, as *al, ar, an*, or *am*. (The vowel sound was faintly pronounced, as in English *button* or *bottom*. *Atalanta* is thus written *Atlnta*, with a sonant *l*, as in English *castle*.)[56]

THE INITIAL STRESS ACCENT AND ITS RESULT

We have seen that Etruscan began to be written around 700 B.C., and was spoken in Italy before that date. Around 500 B.C. or even earlier, a great change took place in the way both Etruscan and Latin were pronounced, when the so-called initial stress accent came into Etruscan and Latin (as well as other languages of Italy). At this time all words were heavily stressed, or accented, on the first syllable. The rest of the word was proportionately less stressed, and vowels dropped out ('syncope'), or were replaced by 'weaker' vowels, less strongly pronounced. An example will show most clearly the nature of this intensive, or stress, accent. In a bilingual text (p. 59), the Latin word *praesentis* (*praesentes*) is rendered in Etruscan as *preśnts*. The Etruscan word has lost two vowels as a result of an intensive initial accent which caused the first syllable to be heavily stressed: the following vowels received proportionately less stress, gradually weakened, and eventually dropped out altogether. This stress accent, which caused such vowels to drop out, was stronger in Etruscan than in Latin, and its results are most obvious in the later Etruscan or 'Neo-Etruscan' inscriptions of the Hellenistic or Roman period.

In Etruscan we find, for example, the Greek name *Aléxandros* (used to refer to Paris Alexander) written in an abbreviated form, *Alcsentre*; and an even more abbreviated form, *Elcsntre*. There are many other examples: *Ramutha* (a woman's name) becomes *Ramtha*; *Rasenna* (the name of the Etruscans) becomes *Rasna*; *Menerva* (Minerva) becomes *Menrva*; *Klytaimestra* (Clytemnestra) becomes *Clutumsta*, then *Clutmsta*; *turice* becomes *turce*; *amake* becomes *amuce*, then *amce*.[57]

The pronunciation of English gives us a number of examples of such syncope: *Leicester* and *Worcester* are both pronounced in a 'syncopated' way. The origin of the word 'alms' in English was Latin *eleēmosyna*, Greek *eleēmosýnē*.

Final vowels are also frequently dropped because of the initial accent, as happens quite regularly in Germanic words in English: *suthithi* becomes *suthith*, 'in the grave'.

CHAPTER V

GRAMMAR

Etruscan, like Latin, uses various inflections or changes of ending for nouns, pronouns, and verbs. We can, in fact, set up a systematic, though incomplete, description of Etruscan grammar. For the sake of clarity, and to show the relationship between the Etruscan inscription and the translation, specific examples will be used to illustrate each point.

NOUNS

Personal names have gender in Etruscan; common nouns do not. Both types of nouns are, however, regularly declined. There are different forms for the different case endings, according to the function of the noun in the sentence.[58]

Many endings are the same for the singular and the plural. Often, however, the plural is formed by adding the suffix *-ar, -er,* or *-ur.* So we have *clan,* 'son' (sing.), and *clenar,* 'sons' (plu.).[59]

As in other languages, with numerals the plural has no special form, but is identical to the singular, as for example, in *ci avil,* 'three years', or *śa śuthi cerichunce,* '(he) built four tombs'.

Here are sample declensions:[60]

	Singular	Plural
Nominative or Accusative	*clan,* 'son'	*clenar,* 'the sons'
Genitive ('of' or 'to')	*clans,* 'of the son'	
Dative	*clenśi,* 'to the son'	*clenaraśi, cliniiaras,* 'to
Locative ('in' or 'at')	**clenthi,* 'in the son'	the sons'[61]

	Singular	Plural
Nominative or Accusative	*śpura, 'city'	*śpurer[62]
Genitive	śpureś, śpural	*śpurerś
Dative	*śpure	
Definite Accusative	śpureni	*śpureri
Locative	śpurethi	

	Singular	Plural
Nominative or Accusative	methlum, 'nation', 'district'	methlumer
Genitive	methlumeś	methlumerś
Definite Accusative	*methlumi	methlumeri
Dative	*methlumśi, methlumale	
Locative	methlumthi	*methlumerthi

In the same way, the plural of *flere*, 'sacred statue', is *flereri*.

There is also an archaic genitive in -*n* (-*an*, -*un*): so *lautn*: gen. *lautun* or *lautn*; *puia*: gen. *puian*.

Those nouns whose stem ends in a velar or dental frequently have a genitive in -(*a*)*l*: *zilach*: *zilachal*; *mech*: *mechl*; *murś*: *murśal*.

	tinś, tin, 'day', 'Jupiter'
Nominative or Accusative	
Genitive	tinśin (archaic)
Dative(?)	tinśi

The -*s*- genitive is frequently added to the stem by means of an euphonic vowel: *śech*: *śechis*; *zathrum*: *zathrumis*; *vel*: *velus*; *venel*: *venelus*; *velthur*: *velthurus*; *clenar*: *clenaras*. Thus:

l(a)ris pulenas larces clan [. . .] *tarchnalth* [. . .]*lucaircе* (*TLE* 131; sarcophagus of Laris Pulenas, Tarquinia). 'Laris Pulenas the son of Larce [. . .] in Tarquinia governed' ('Laris Pulenas, son of Larce, governed in Tarquinia')

auleśi metelis ve(lus) vesial clenśi flereś tece [. . .] (*TLE* 651; statue of the Arringatore, near Perugia, c. 100 B.C.) 'For Aulus Metellius, the son of Vel and Vesi, this statue placed [. . .] ('(He) placed this statue in honour of Aulus Metellius, the son of Vel and Vesi [. . .]')

ci clenar [. . .] *anavence* (*TLE* 98; on a tomb wall, Tarquinia) 'three sons [. . .] she bore' ('She bore three sons')

tular spural [. . .] (*TLE* 675; stone cippus from Fiesole) 'the boundaries of the city . . .'

mi titasi cver menache (*TLE* 282; on the border of a mirror, from Bomarzo, c. 300 B.C.) 'I to Tita as a gift was offered ' ('I was offered as a gift to Tita')

aninas vel velus [. . .] *sa śuthi cerichun(ce)* [. . .](*TLE* 882; wall of a tomb in Tarquinia, third or second century B.C.) 'Aninas Vel (the son) of Vel . . . four tombs built' ('Aninas Vel, the son of Vel, built four tombs . . .')

A special case deserves our attention. The word *avil*, 'year', which occurs very frequently (over 100 times), in funerary inscriptions, is found with the simple stem (*avil*) when it is used with the verbs *svalce* or *svalthas*, meaning 'to live'. With *lupu*, 'dead', we have instead *avils*. This shows that *avil* indicates a continuous action, 'he lived for so many years . . .', while *avils* expresses a precise action or occurrence, 'he died in such-and-such a year':[63]

arnth apunas velus [. . .] *mach cezpalch avil svalce* (*TLE* 94; Tomba Bruschi, Tarquinia, second century B.C.) 'Arnth Apunas (the son) of Vel . . . lived eighty-five years'

velthur larisal clan cuclnial thanchvilus lupu avils XXV (*TLE* 129; sarcophagus from Tarquinia) 'Velthur, the son of Laris (and) of Tanaquil Cuclni, died at twenty-five years'

PROPER NOUNS

Various Etruscan names of gods are known from our sources, especially in the engraved decoration on the backs of mirrors, and on the bronze liver from Piacenza. *Tin* corresponds to the Latin *Iuppiter* or *Jupiter*, and to the Greek *Zeus*; *Fufluns* to *Bacchus* or *Dionysos*; *Uni* to *Iuno* (*Juno*) or *Hera*; *Catha* to *Sol* or *Helios*, 'the Sun'; *Selvans* is *Silvanus* (the Etruscan name perhaps comes from the Latin). Many other Etruscan names refer to gods completely unknown to us. (See the Study Aids: List of Mythological Figures.) On the other hand, in the tombs, on many mirrors, and elsewhere, names of gods are often in Greek: thus *Aita* = *Haides* (Hades), *Phersipnai* = *Persephone* or Latin *Proserpina, Tinas clenar* ('sons of *Tinia*') = the *Dioskouroi* ('sons of Zeus').

Names of gods frequently have a mysterious nominative in -*s*: *cilens, fufluns, tinś, selvans.*

We can learn a great deal about Etruscan phonetics, as we have seen, from the way the Etruscans transcribed these Greek names. There are also many cases when we have both the Latin and Etruscan equivalents of a name.

Personal names in Etruscan, unlike common nouns, have the gender clearly indicated: the masculine ends in a consonant or -*e*; the feminine usually in -*a* or -*i*. The Greek name of one of the three Fates, *Atropos*, is written *athrpa* on a bronze mirror, for example, with an ending in -*a* (fig. 25).

masculine	feminine
aule	*aula*
vel	*vela*
sethre	*sethra*
arnth	*arnthi*
larth	*larthi*

The genitive ends in -*al* or -*s* or -*us* (for both masculine and feminine,[64] after a liquid consonant, as for example *vel-us* masc. and *thanchvil-us* fem.).[65] A special ending, -*sa* or -*isa*, is sometimes found replacing the word 'son', and therefore indicates a patronymic, 'son of'. The following two phrases are therefore equivalent: *aule velimna larthal clan* = *aule velimna larthalisa* 'Aulus Velimna, son of Larth' (from the tomb of the Volumnii, Perugia).

nominative	genitive	patronymic
larth	*larthal*	*larthalisa*
arnth	*arnthal*	*arnthalisa*
laris	*larisal*	*larisalisa*

In early times, in the seventh century B.C. in Etruria, as in Rome, *one* name only was used; Etruscan *Aranth, Larth, Venel, Mamarce*, etc. (Latin *Rōmulus, Rēmus, Amulius, Numitor*, etc.). Later, during the last years of the seventh century, a formula of two names developed (as is customary today in most countries): a personal name and a family name (called, in Latin, the *nomen gentile*). The family name in Etruscan usually has the adjectival suffix -*na* (under Italic influence, also -*ie* from -*ios*, -*ius*): *avile vipiiennas* (*TLE* 35), *larth paithunas* (TLE 256), *avle larchnas* (CIE 5914), *laris tarnas* (CIE 5904). Frequently the name of the father is also added: *avle tarchnas larthal clan* (CIE 5904); sometimes (but much less often) the name of the mother is placed after the father's name: *laris tarnas velus clan ranthasc matunial herma* (CIE 5904).

In this last inscription we also find, as in Rome, the third name or *cognōmen*. We have, then: (a) the personal name (*laris*); (b) the family name or *nōmen gentīle* (*tarnas*); (c) the patronymic (*velus clan* — the son of *Vel*, gen. *Velus*); (d) the matronymic (*ranthas-c*); (e) the mother's patronymic (*matun-ial* = the daughter of *matun*); (f) the *cognōmen* (*herma*). It is not clear whether the three-name system is of Etruscan or Latin origin.

The new organization of the Etruscans within a city model requires a new distinction of persons, since the patronymic system is no longer sufficient. In this context the new system of the family name is created (even though the use of the patronymic is not completely dropped). A similar change occurred once more, much later, in Europe. In a rural society, during the Middle Ages, one name was long sufficient; but around the year 1300, with the growing importance of city life, the family name developed again. Dante's great-grandfather, *Cacciaguida*, had only one name. Dante had two: *Dante Alighieri*, as he specifically tells us in the *Divine Comedy* (*Par.* XV, 91; 138).

A special double genitive indicated the grandfather, as does the name O'Connor in Irish. Thus a man is called *aule velimna larthal*, 'Aulus Velimna, son of Larth'. His son will be *arnth velimna aules*, 'Arnth Velimna, son of Aulus'. In important families the grandfather's name Larth will also be mentioned, with the special ending, *-sa* or *-sla*: *arnth velimna aules clan larthalisla*, because Larth is the father of Aule and therefore the grandfather of Arnth.

Personal names also have a dative in *-la* or *-iale* (*vestiricinala*, dative of *vestiricinai*), aside from the dative in *-si* (*titasi, hulchniesi*).

There also seems to be a special case of the 'agent':

nominative	genitive	agent
tarna	*tarnas*	*tarnes*
ramtha	*ramthas*	*ramthes*
vel	*velus*	*veluis*
thanchvil	*thanchvilus*	*thanchviluis*

thanchvil tarna an farthnache marces tarnes ramthesc chaireals (TLE 321; sarcophagus from Vulci) 'Tanaquil Tarnai: she was buried by Marcus Tarna and Ramtha (the daughter of) Chairei'.

Names of gods, unlike other personal names, often have no gender. We have no way of knowing from the form of the name whether *Tin, Turan, Pacha, Uni, Vanth,* or *Aplu* are male or female divinities. The males sometimes may have a nominative ending in *-s*: thus we have *cilen* and *cilens*, *fuflun* and *fufluns*, *tin* and *tins*, *selvan* and *selvans*. The same nominative in ⸍*s* is found in common nouns, added to the genitive form, for example *papals*, 'the one of the grandfather', that is 'the grandfather's grandson'; *tetals*, 'the one of the grandmother', or 'the grandmother's grandson'; *truials*, from *truial* (genitive), 'of Troy', therefore 'the one from Troy', referring to a Trojan prisoner in the François tomb (source 43; fig. 35).⁶⁶

Family names, probably ancient patronymics, as in Latin and other languages, are formed with ⸍*na* in Etruscan.

first name	family name	
	archaic	later form
ar(a)nth	**ar(n)thena*	*arnthna*
thuker	*thucerna*	
laucie	*laucina*	*lucina*
pumpu	*pumpuna*	*pumpna*
puplie	**pupliena*	*puplina*
spurie	**spuriena*	*spurina* (whence Latin *Spurinna*)

Several first names ending in ⸍*ie* in Etruscan are obviously of Latin or Italic origin, for example: *spurie* from *Spurius*; *kae* from *Caius* (the *i* disappears between two vowels); *laucie* from *Lucius* (originally *Loucios* in Latin); *puplie* from *Publius*.

In southern Etruria, the family name, which eventually simply corresponded to our modern last names, such as 'Smith' or 'Jones', has an added ⸍*s*: thus *avile vipiiennas* (*TLE* 35; in an inscription from Veii, dating from about 550 B.C.), and *larth alethnas* (*TLE* 172; from Musarna, near Tarquinia, second century B.C.).

PRONOUNS

Personal pronouns

First person

mi–'I' (nominative)

mi culichna [. . .] *Venelus* (*TLE* 3; on an Attic red⸍figure cup from Capua, *c.* 475 B.C.): 'I (am) the cup [. . .] of Venel'

The verb 'to be' can be omitted, a feature of grammar found in many ancient languages, including Greek and Latin. In addition, it may be noted that the cup is speaking for itself, as though it were animated: this, too, is a frequent feature in ancient languages like Greek and Latin.

velchaie pustminas mi (*TLE* 22; vase, Campanian) 'Of Velchaie Pustmina I (am)' ('I belong to Velchaie Pustmina')

mini—'me' (accusative)
mini muluvanece avile vipiiennas (*TLE* 35; on a bucchero cup from Veii, *c.* 550 B.C.) 'me offered Aulus Vibenna' ('Aulus Vibenna offered me')
mini turuce larth apunas velethnalas (*TLE* 760; on a pitcher, bucchero oinochoe, uncertain provenance) 'me gave Lars Apunas to Velethna' ('Lars Apunas gave me to Velethna'). *Velethnalas*, a dative, has a mysterious *s*.

Second person
We do not know the form for the second person, because it appears in none of our texts.

Third person
There is only one personal pronoun for 'he', 'she', or 'it'. Etruscan makes no distinction in gender between male and female forms, but there is, perhaps, a distinction between animate and inanimate (i.e. the neuter): *an* is for persons, *in* for objects.

vel matunas larisalisa an cn śuthi cerichunce (*TLE* 51; cippus from Cerveteri) 'Vel Matunas (the son) of Laris he this tomb built' ('Vel Matunas, the son of Laris, he built this tomb')

. . . *Spurinas an zilath amce* . . . (*TLE* 87; *Elogia Tarquiniensia*, first century A.D.) '. . . Spurinna; he praetor was . . .' ('. . . Spurinna; he was praetor . . .').

Demonstrative pronouns
For the demonstrative pronoun 'this' we find either *ca* or *ta* used, without any apparent difference between the two words. The following forms are found:

	Singular	Plural
Nominative or Accusative	eca, ca, ta	cai, tei
Genitive	cla, tla	clal
Accusative	cehen	cnl
	cen, cn,	
	etan, or tn	

Locative	*calti*	*caiti*
	clth(i)	*ceithi*

For example:

Nominative

By the doors of tombs

ca śuthi   *ta śuthi*

'this (is) the grave'   'this (is) the grave'

On a bronze mirror, incised next to a picture of the chariot of the sun
(*TLE* 340; from Orbetello):

ca thesan

'this (is) the dawn'

Genitive

On the mummy wrappings from Zagreb (*TLE* 1 [5.23]. Source 54, fig.
38):

cla thesan [. . .]

'of (during) this morning [. . .]' ('in day light')

lautn velthinaś eśtla afunaś (*TLE* 570 [1], cippus of Perugia)

'freedman of (belonging to) the family Velthina and of this (family)
Afuna'

Accusative

cn turce murila hercnas [. . .] (*TLE* 149; bronze staff from Tarquinia)

'this gave Murila Hercnas' ('Murila Hercnas gave this')

[. . .] *cen fleres tece* [. . .] (*TLE* 651; bronze statue of Arringatore from
Perugia)

'[. . .] this statue placed [. . .]' ('[. . .] placed this statue [. . .]')

tn turce ramtha uftatavi selvan (*TLE* 696; bronze statuette of a man, from
Carpegna in Umbria)

'This gave Ramtha Uftavi to Selvan' ('Ramtha Uftavi gave this to
Silvanus'). The writer has written *uftatavi* instead of *uftavi*.

Locative

thui clthi mutniathi [. . .] (*TLE* 93; Tomba Bruschi, Tarquinia, second
century B.C.)

'here in this sarcophagus [. . .]'

calti śuthiti (*TLE* 135; sarcophagus from Tarquinia).

'in this grave'

It may be noted that all cases save the nominative are formed from the stem (*cal* or *cl*), as is frequently to be seen in Indoeuropean languages. When such a pronoun is attached to the end of a noun, as an enclitic, it is used as an article. So, on the Zagreb mummy wrappings (*TLE* 1) we find *sacni⁓cn*, or *sacni⁓tn*, 'the priest'.

Other forms of the demonstrative have an initial vowel:

Nominative	*ika* (archaic)	*eca* (later form)
	ita	
Accusative	*ikan* (archaic)	*ecn* (later form)
	itan, itun	
Locative	*eclthi*	

For example:

Nominative
   eca mutana cutus velus (*TLE* 115; on a sarcophagus from Tarquinia, second century B.C.)
   'This (is) the sarcophagus of Cutu Vel'
   eca sren tva [. . .] (*TLE* 399; on a mirror from Volterra, *c.* 300 B.C.) (Source No. 26, fig. 20).
   'This image shows [. . .]'

Accusative
   ecn turce larthi lethanei [. . .] (*TLE* 559; Neo⁓Etruscan; bronze statuette of a man)
   'This gave Larthi Lethanei [. . .]' ('Larthi Lethanei gave this [. . .]')
   itan mulvanice th[. . .] (*TLE* 39; bucchero oinochoe from Veii)
   'This offered Th . . .' (an individual) ('Th . . . offered this')
   itun turuce venel atelinas tinas cliniiaras (*TLE* 156; Attic red⁓figure cup from Tarquinia, *c.* 475 B.C.)
   'This gave Venel Atelinas to Tin's sons' ('Venel Atelinas gave this to the sons of Jupiter' – i.e., to the Dioskouroi, Castor and Pollux).

Locative
   eclthi ramtha cainei (*TLE* 276; sarcophagus from Ferento, Southern Etruria)
   'In this (sarcophagus) (is) Ramtha Cainei' ('Here lies Ramtha Cainei')
   eclthi śuthith larth zalthu . . . (*TLE* 116; grave stone from Tarquinia)
   'In this grave (is) Lars Zalthu . . .'

There are thus two series: *ita, eta, ta*; and also *ica, eca, ca*.

The relative pronoun 'who', 'which' is *ipa*, which is indeclinable, like English 'that', Italian *che*. The indefinite, 'whoever', is *ipe ipa* (probably from *ipa ipa*; compare the Latin word for 'whoever', *quisquis*, related to the relative pronoun *qui*.)

We do not know the form of the interrogative pronoun, since there are no dialogues, in which it would be used.

NUMERALS

Etruscan numerals have long presented a difficult problem. Progress has recently been made, thanks in part to the new discoveries from Pyrgi. We have the good fortune to have a set of dice (now in Paris) on which the numbers are written out in words, spelled phonetically, not in figures (fig. 7). We therefore know for certain the numbers from 1 to 6.[67] These numbers also appear in many funerary inscriptions, indicating the age of the deceased. The numbers are *thu, zal, ci, śa, mach, huth*. The problem is, which is 1, which is 2, and so on? We know that among the ancients the two

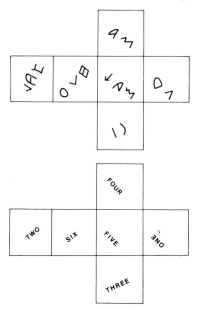

7 Inscribed Etruscan names of numerals on ivory dice, with English translation. Hellenistic period

opposite faces of a die add up to 7,[68] $mach + zal = 7$, $thu + huth = 7$, $ci + śa = 7$. Yet this still does not tell us what the value of each number is, for $mach + zal$ could be $1 + 6$, or $2 + 5$, or $3 + 4$. An early investigator, the Danish scholar Torp, theorized that the numbers were as follows: $thu = 1$; $zal = 2$; $ci = 3$; $śa = 4$; $mach = 5$; $huth = 6$. His theory has received confirmation from the inscriptions on the Pyrgi tablets (fig. 5, p. 54), which give us the value of *ci* beyond any possible doubt, for the word is repeated three times: we have *ci avil* on one of the Etruscan tablets, and, in the Phoenician inscription, the symbol III as well as the Phoenician translation *šlš* meaning 'three'. Knowing that $ci = 3$, we also know that *śa* is 4, because $ci + śa$ (or $3 + 4$) $= 7$.

The numeral 10 is **śar* (*huth-zar* is 'sixteen', and *śar-vena* is *decem-uir*, 'one of a committee of ten'). The numeral 20 is *zathrum* (related to *za-* or *sa-*, 'two'). Above 10, counting proceeds by addition as far as 6 (for instance, *huthis zathrumiś*, 'on the twenty-sixth [day]'), and by subtraction from 7 to 9 (for example *esl-em-zathrumiś*, 'on the twentieth minus two', that is 'on the eighteenth [day]'. *TLE* 1).

Multiples of 10 are formed by adding *-alc* or *-alch*. (Asterisked forms are reconstructed.)

Forming numerals by subtraction is a highly unusual system, found only in Etruscan and in Latin. $18 = 20 - 2$, $19 = 20 - 1$: Latin *duodēuīgintī*, *undēuīgintī* ('eighteen', 'nineteen'). The Roman system was probably due to Etruscan influence.[69]

1	*thu*	20	*zathrum*
2	*zal (esal)*	23	*ci zathrum*
3	*ci*	27	*ci-em-ce-alch*
4	*śa*	28	*esl-em-ce-alch*
5	*mach*	29	*thun-em-ce-alch*
6	*huth*	30	*ci-alch (ce-alch)*
7	*semph* (?)	40	*se-alch*
8	*cezp* (?)	50	*muv-alch (*mach-alch)*
9	*nurph* (?)	60	**huth-alch*
10	**śar*	70	*semph-alch* (?)
13	**ci-śar*	80	*cezp-alch* (?)
16	*huth-zar*	90	**nurph-alch* (?)
17	*ci-em zathrum*	100	?
18	*esl-em zathrum*	1000	?
19	*thun-em zathrum*		

Numerals are declined like nouns:

Nominative or accusative	*thu(n), zal, ci, mach, huth, semph* (?)
Genitive	*thuns̓, esals, cis̓, machs, huthis, semphs* (?)
Definite accusative	*thuni*
Locative	*thuni*

When numerals are compounds both elements are inflected. In the genitive, we have *cis̓ s̓aris̓,* 'on the thirteenth', *huthis̓ zathrumis̓,* 'on the twenty-sixth'. Only the subtractive element (*em*) and the numeral that precedes it are indeclinable. So on the mummy wrappings we have *eslem zathrumis̓ acale,* 'on the eighteenth (day) of June'; *thunem cialchus,* 'on the twenty-ninth', *ciem cealchus,* 'on the twenty-seventh'.

Ordinals are formed with the suffix *-na* (see below, Adjectives): *thuns̓na,* 'the first'.

Special numeral adverbs are formed with the ending *-zi* or *-z: thunz,* 'once', *eslz,* 'twice', *ciz,* 'three times', *huthz,* 'six times', *cezpz,* 'eight times' (?), *nurphzi,* 'nine times' (?), etc. These adverbs are used to record the number of magistracies held by public officials:

larth ceisinis velus clan cizi zilachnce methlum nurphzi canthce (*TLE* 99; Tarquinia, wall painting) 'Lars Ceisini, the son of Vel, three times as praetor governed the district, (and) nine (?) times was censor'.

tute arnthals [. . .] *zilchnu cezpz purts̓vana thunz lupu avils esals cezpalchals* (*TLE* 324; man's sarcophagus from Vulci, second century B.C.) 'Tute, (the son) of Arnth, having been praetor eight times, dictator once, (was) dead in the year eighty-two (of his life)'

There is also a distributive ending: *thunur,* 'one at a time'; *zelur,* 'two at a time', etc.

ADJECTIVES

There are three types of adjectives in Etruscan.

I Adjectives of quality

(*a*)   Ending in *-u* or *-iu* (*i* disappears between vowels):

ais, 'god'	*aisiu,* 'godly', 'divine'
hinth, 'below'	*hinthiu,* 'underground', 'infernal'
etera, 'stranger', 'client', 'slave'	*eterau,* 'connected with an *etera*'
*s̓arsnach, 'tenth'	*s̓ars̓nau,* 'a group of ten', or 'decuria'

(b) Ending in ⸗c:

zamathi, 'gold'	zamthic, 'golden'
*athumi, 'nobility'	athumic, 'noble'

II Adjectives of possession or reference

Ending in ⸗na:

ais, eis, 'god'	aisna, eisna, 'pertaining to a god', divine'
lauchumu, 'magistrate', 'lucumo'	lauchumna, 'pertaining to a magistrate', or 'lucumo'
*pacha, 'Bacchus'	pachana, 'pertaining or belonging to Bacchus'
śpura, 'city'	śpurana, 'pertaining or belonging to the city'
śuthi, 'tomb', 'grave'	śuthina, 'pertaining or belonging to the grave', 'grave gift'
thunś, 'one'	thunśna, 'first'

The suffixes ⸗na, ⸗ne, ⸗ni, indicating adjectives derived from both proper names (of persons or places) and common nouns, are certainly related to this class of adjectives. Family names or *nomina gentilia* belong to this group. We see, for example, the names *velthurna* from *velthur*; *vipina* from *vipi*; *papni* from *papa*, 'grandfather'; *lautni*, 'freedman', from *laut*, 'family', etc.

III Adjectives expressing a collective idea

Ending in ⸗cva (⸗cve), ⸗va, ⸗ia:

math, 'inebriating drink'	math⸗cva, 'full of inebriating drink'
sren, 'ornament'	sren⸗cve, 'full of ornament'
avil, 'year'	avil⸗cva, 'perennial' (compare Latin perennis = per + annos)
purth, title of magistracy	eprthieva, 'connected with the *purth*'
raśna, 'Etruria', 'the Etruscan people'	raśna⸗ia, 'connected with the Etruscans'
etera, 'stranger', 'client', 'slave	etera⸗ia, 'connected with the *etera*'

After a liquid consonant (*l, r, m, n*) the *c* may become *ch*: *sren⸗chve*, 'full of ornament', *fler⸗chva*, 'group of sacred statues', sacrifice.

This ending forms words denoting collective plurals, which exist alongside the usual individual plural forms: so, for example, from *flere*, 'sacred statue', comes the individualizing plural *flereri*, 'sacred statues', as well as the collective plural *flerchva*, 'a group of sacred statues'[70] (cf. Latin *locus*, sing., *loci, loca*, pl.).

As in other languages, several suffixes or endings may be used in combination: see, for example, *sarsnau, purtsvau, eprthneva, purtsvana, sarvena, zelarvena*.

Adjectives are as a rule indeclinable, unless they are used as nouns (as in English).

tarchnal-thi, 'in Tarquinii' (pl.); *velsnal-thi*, 'in Volsinii' (pl.).

VERBS

We do not know the verbal forms for the first and second persons, 'I' and 'you', with the exception of the past passive (*-che*, the passive form, is used for both the first and the third persons). The third person seems to have been the same in the singular and plural. We can recognize a number of verbal forms, however.

I Finite Verbs

(a) Active – present
Either the radical form is used (*ar, rach, tur, puth*, etc.), or a form with an ending in *-a* (*ara, ama, tva*).

eca sren tva (*TLE* 399) 'This image shows . . .'

(b) Active – preterite
There are many words ending in *-ce* (or *-ke*).[71] These all indicate a third person singular form of the past tense of the verb. We have already come upon a number of these, as for example:

itun turuce venel atelinas tinas cliniiaras (*TLE* 156; Attic red-figure cup from Tarquinia, *c.* 475 B.C.) 'This gave Venel Atelinas to Tin's sons' ('Venel Atelinas gave this to the sons of Jupiter')

The later, shortened form of *turuce* is *turce*.

Here are some other examples:

papalser acnanasa VI manim arce (*TLE* 169; man's sarcophagus from Musarna) 'Having acquired six grandchildren he elevated the monument'

('He had six grandchildren, and built this monument')

mini muluvanice mamarce apuniie venala (*TLE* 34; bucchero pitcher from Veii) 'Me dedicated Mamercus Apunie Venala' ('Mamercus Apunie Venala dedicated me')

mini urthanike aranthur (*TLE* 764; bucchero cup, provenance unknown) 'Me made Aranthur' ('Aranthur made me')

The past ending of the third person -*ce* was used for both the singular and the plural. For the singular, see, for example, *vel matunas* [. . .] *cn śuthi cerchunce* 'Vel Mathunas built (sing.) this tomb' (*TLE* 51). In a new inscription[72] we read: *laris avle larisal clenar* [. . .] *cn suthi cerichunce* 'Laris (and) Aulus, sons of Laris, built this tomb', where 'built', obviously a plural, has the same ending as the singular (as in English and other modern languages).

(c) Active − future (?)
A form in -*ne* is probably a future, in the third person:

mi murs arnthal veteś nufreś laris vete mulune la(r)thia petruni mulune (*TLE* 420; cinerary urn from Poggibonsi). 'I am the urn of Arnth Vete Nufre. Laris Vete will offer. Larthia Petronia will offer'.

velthina acilune turune ścune (*TLE* 570; cippus from Perugia), 'Velthina will do, give, yield'

(d) Passive − preterite
While the ending -*ce* indicates the active preterite, the ending -*che* seems to indicate the passive preterite for the first person singular:[73]

mi arathiale zichuche (*TLE* 278; bucchero aryballos) 'I for Arath was written' 'I was written for Arath'

mi titasi cver menache (*TLE* 282; bronze mirror from Bomarzo, *c.* 300 B.C.) 'I was offered as a gift to Tita'[74]

II Passive participles − past participle or verbal noun

If we compare two inscriptions, both dating from approximately 600 B.C., we can see that one has an active verb, the other a passive:

mini alice velthur (*TLE* 43; bucchero vase from Veii) 'Me gave Velthur' ('Velthur gave me')

can be compared with:

mi spurieisi teithurnasi aliqu (*TLE* 940; bucchero kylix, uncertain provenance) 'I to Spurie Teithurna was given'

Since *mi* is the nominative, the form *aliqu* must be a passive verb. We therefore translate the second sentence as, 'I (was) given to Spurius Teithurna'. So too:

mi lartuzale kuleniiesi zinaku (*SE* 1972, *REE* 1; from Artimino, *c.* 600 B.C.) 'I for Larthuza Kulenie (was) made' 'I (was) made for Larthuza Kulenie'

These forms in *u* seem to be past participles. If the verb is transitive, the meaning is passive: *mulu*, 'offered'; *turu*, 'given' (from the roots *mul-* and *tur-*). If the verb is intransitive, the meaning is active: *lupu*, 'dead', or *cesu*, 'lying'.

larth auclina cesu thui (*TLE* 553; urn, near Chiusi) 'Lars Auclina (is) lying here' ('Here lies Lars Auclina'; or, in Latin, *hic iacet*)

mi licinesi mulu hirsunaiesi (*TLE* 769; Corinthian alabastron, uncertain provenance) 'I to Licinius Hirsunaie (was) offered' 'I (was) offered to Licinius Hirsunaie'

A verb which occurs frequently in funerary inscriptions is *lupu*, 'dead', or the related form *lupuce*. It is used with the noun *avils*, 'year', to mean 'died' (at a certain age):[75] *avils LXX lupu* 'In (his) seventieth year he (was) dead'; or *avils LX lupuce* 'He died (at the age of) sixty years'.

This active preterite participle ending in -*u* is very close to that of the verbal form in -*ce*, together with which it is often used:

semni ramtha spitus larthal puia amce lupu avils XXII husur ci acnanas (*TLE* 889; wall of tomb in Tarquinia, second century B.C.) 'Semni Ramtha of Spitus (the son) of Lars was the wife; (she was) dead in the twenty-second year (of her life); three children she had.' ('Semni Ramtha was the wife of Spitus, the son of Lars; she died when she was twenty-two years old, having had three children'.)

III Active Participles

(*a*) There is an active past participle (preterite) ending in ⸗*thas*. Compare, for example: *avil svalthas I.XXXII* (*TLE* 126) 'having lived eighty⸗two years', with *svalce avil XXVI* 'He lived (during) twenty⸗six years'. Or: *eslz zilachnthas* (*TLE* 136; sarcophagus from Tarquinia, third century B.C.) 'having been praetor twice', with *cizi zilachnce* (*TLE* 99; Tomba Bruschi, Tarquinia, second century B.C.) 'Three times he was praetor'.

(*b*) Another active past participle ends in ⸗*asa*:

clenar ci acnanasa elsśi zilachnu (*TLE* 169; man's sarcophagus from Musarna) 'sons three having procreated, for the second time he was praetor' ('Having procreated three sons, he was praetor for the second time')

(*c*) Another participle ending in ⸗*as* expresses contemporary action, something like English 'living', 'doing':

spurethi apasi svalas (*TLE* 171; man's sarcophagus from Musarna) 'While living in the city of his father (?) . . .'

vacl aras thui useti (*TLE* 1.10.18; the Zagreb mummy) '(While) making the libation, draw (from) here'

(*d*) A present participle is formed with an ending ⸗*an*: *mulvan*, 'founding', *turan*, 'giving', *alpan*, 'willing(ly)'.

V(elia) cvinti arntiaś culśanśl alpan turce (*TLE* 640; bronze statuette of double⸗faced divinity, from Cortona, fourth or third century B.C.) (Source 38; fig. 32) 'Velia Quintia, (the daughter) of Arnth, to (the god) Culsans willing(ly) gave' ('Velia Quintia, the daughter of Arnth, willingly gave (this) to the god Culsans'.) (Cf. Latin *d.d.l.* = *donum dedit libens*, 'gave the gift willingly' – the same formula, and a good example of Pallottino's method, the 'cultural approach' mentioned earlier.)

(*e*) A participle denoting obligation is formed with the ending ⸗*(e)ri*:

huthiś zathrumiśflerchva nethunsl [. . .] *thezeri⸗c* (*TLE* 1.8.3; Zagreb mummy wrappings) 'and on the twenty⸗sixth the sacrifices for Neptune are to be made'

IV Imperative

(a) Imperative I

The simple verbal stem can be used as an imperative form (as in the Indoeuropean languages, e.g. Latin *cantā*, 'sing', etc.). For example, *vacl ar* 'Make the libation' (*ar* = 'make', 'do').

(b) Imperative II

Another imperative, ending in ⸗ti, ⸗th or ⸗thi, and used for the second person is also found in the text inscribed on the mummy wrappings from Zagreb.

hathrthi repinthi⸗c śacnicleri cilthl śpureri methlumeri⸗c enaś śveleri⸗c 'Be benevolent and bow to the temples of the people, to the cities and districts and hearths'

rachth tura(,) nunthenth cletram śrenchve tei faśei 'Prepare the incense, offer with the decorated cup these breads'

tur rachti 'Prepare the incense'
(All these imperatives come from the Zagreb mummy wrappings, *TLE* 1.)

Verb synopses

	mul⸗ 'dedicate'	tur⸗ 'give'	sval⸗ 'live'	zich⸗ 'write'	rach⸗ 'prepare'
3rd singular indicative	*mula*	*tura*			
imperative I		*tur*			*rach*
imperative II					*rachti, rachth*
present participle	*mulvan*	*turan*	*svalas*		
past participle or verbal noun	*mulu*	*turu*		*zichu*	
participle of obligation		*turi*			
		(tur + ri)			
past active		*turce*	*svalce*		
participle of the preterite			*svalthas*		
future?	*mulune*	*turune*			
passive 1st person				*zichuche*	

CONJUNCTIONS AND ADVERBS

Coordinate Conjunctions

⸗*c* is 'and' (after *l* it is often written *ch*). It is added, as an enclitic, after both nouns which are being connected, or else only after the second noun. When there are three nouns it can be placed after the first one. (Compare the Latin ending ⸗*que* meaning 'and'.) Hence:

apac atic (CIE 6213) 'both father and mother'

marces tarnes ramthesc chaireals (*TLE* 321; sarcophagus from Vulci with figures of husband and wife reclining together) 'for Marcus Tarna and

Ramtha Chairei'

ᵐ (⸍um after a consonant) also means 'and':

ramtha matulnai [. . .] *ci clenar* [. . .] *anavence lupu⸍m avils machs śealchlsc* (*TLE* 98; wall of tomb, Tarquinia, second century B.C.) 'Ramtha Matulnai [. . .] three sons she bore and (was) dead in the forty⸍fifth year (of her life)'

vel leinies larthial ruva arnthialum clan velusum prumathś [. . .] (*TLE* 232; painted over figure of a serving boy, in Tomba Golini I, Sette Camini, near Orvieto, fourth century B.C.) 'Vel Leinies, brother of Lars and son of Arnth and great⸍grandson of Vel'

Sometimes the conjunction is left out (asyndeton):

arnth larth velimnaś arzneal husiur [. . .] (*TLE* 566; Tomba dei Volumnii, Perugia, second or first century B.C.) 'Arnth (and) Lars Velimnas, children of Arzni'

Other conjunctions and adverbs

sve, 'likewise'
ic, ich, 'as'
ichnac, 'how'
etnam, 'also'
ratum, 'accurately'

Adverbs of time (temporal)

thuni, 'at first' (cf. *thu,* 'one')
etnam, 'again'
(e)nac, 'then', 'after'
matam, 'before', 'earlier'
epl, pul, 'until'
thui, 'now'
une, 'and then'

Adverbs of place (local)

thui, 'here'
hauthin, 'in front of'
hinththin, 'from below' (with reference to the underworld; cf. *hinthial,* 'shade', 'ghost')
ipa, 'where' (relative)
thar, 'there', 'thither' (motion towards)

SYNTAX

Since long texts are rare and Etruscan literature unknown to us, we do not know much about Etruscan syntax. The little which has been preserved seems not to be very different from that of the Indoeuropean languages (a fact which does not, however, imply any relationship).

Word order is similar to that of Latin. The subject is placed at the beginning, the verbs at the end; but the imperative is usually placed at the beginning.

An important feature which Etruscan shares with some Indoeuropean languages is a so-called 'group inflection', meaning that when there are two nouns, sometimes it is the second one only that receives the case ending:

mamerze (for *mamerce*) *paziathes-mi* (*SE* 42, 1974, 306, No. 284; fifth century B.C.) 'I (am) of (or 'belong to') Mamercus Paziathe' (only *Paziathe* has the genitive case ending *-s*).

The dative is also used with the function of the Latin ablative absolute:

clenśi [. . .] *svalasi* (*TLE* 173; man's sarcophagus from Musarna) 'while the son was living'

larthiale hulchniesi marcesic caliathesi (*TLE* 84; Tarquinia, Tomba dell'Orco, fourth century B.C.) '(In the magistracy of) Larth Hulchnie and Marcus Caliathe'

zilci velusi hulchuniesi (*TLE* 90; Tarquinia, Tomba degli Scudi, third century B.C.)

'At the time when Velus Hulchnie was *zilc*', i.e. a praetor.[76]

This formula in the dative corresponds to the Latin system of dating by consulships in the ablative absolute: *M. Tullio Cicerone oratore et C. Antonio consulibus (62 B.C.)*, 'In the consulship of Marcus Tullius Cicero the orator and of Caius Antonius'. (This was the way of giving a date in Rome; compare the *eponymous archon*, the magistrate after whom the year was named, in Athens.)

VOCABULARY

In the absence of any works of Etruscan literature, our knowledge of Etruscan vocabulary is necessarily limited. The fact that what we have are mostly ritual or religious texts and epitaphs means that there is a good deal of repetition, as well as a large number of proper names, of divinities as well as people. So, although there are some 13,000 inscriptions, we have a vocabulary consisting of about 250 words only. Even some of these are uncertain in meaning. We have, for example, several words meaning 'to give', 'to offer', 'to build', and so on, each of which must have had a more precise meaning.[77]

Yet for several areas there is a good deal of evidence. Names of divinities, as well as religious vocabulary in general (for example *ais*, 'god', pl. *aiser*) are quite well known. Eva Fiesel and Carlo de Simone[78] have studied the way in which Greek names of divinities were transcribed into Etruscan; and we know something about these Greek, as well as other, native divinities, from the way they are represented in art, in wall paintings, or on engraved bronze mirrors (see pp. 147–150).

Two other types of words are also rather well known: numerals, which we know both from epitaphs, with the ages and terms of office of the deceased, and from such a ritual calendar as the mummy wrappings in Zagreb; and nouns indicating the various family relationships. The latter, of course, are found frequently on funerary inscriptions or epitaphs.

Following are some of these terms of family relationships:

clan, 'son' (very frequent)

sech, 'daughter' (fairly frequent)

nefts, nefiś, nefś, 'grandson', 'son of the daughter' (from the Latin word *nepōs*, related to English 'nephew').

prumathś, prumts, 'great-grandson' (from the Latin word *prōnepōs*, 'great-grandson')

papa, 'grandfather'

teta, 'grandmother'

papals, 'grandson', 'the son of the son' (literally, 'he of the grandfather')

puia, 'wife' (very frequent)

husiur, 'children'

ati, 'mother' (there is a form *ativu*, 'Mummy')

apa, 'father'

talitha, 'girl'

ati nacn(u)va, 'grandmother' ('venerable mother'; this is a euphemism, for which compare French *belle-mère, beau-père*, 'beautiful mother', 'handsome father', i.e. 'mother-in-law' and 'father-in-law').

ateri, 'parents', 'ancestors'

ruva, 'brother'

clente, 'adoptive son' (?)

Since Etruscan society was patriarchal, we do not (yet) know the words for 'husband', 'uncle', 'cousin', etc. But new inscriptions are found almost weekly, and our vocabulary is enriched by these new discoveries.

We know the names of a number of magistrates, but their ranks, duties and privileges are not always clear to us. In the translations given we have used, for the sake of convenience, some conventional equivalents. They are listed below according to their approximate relative importance, from highest to lowest.

purth, 'dictator'
lauchume, 'consul' (cf. Latin *lucumō,* 'high priest', 'king', or 'ruler')
zilath, zilch, etc., 'praetor'. (In a bilingual inscription, *zilch cechaneri* is
    translated as *praetor iure dicundo* in Latin; but in the Pyrgi tablet
    (fig. 5) the word means 'ruler', perhaps 'king'.)
camthi, 'censor'
maru, 'Maro' (Umbrian word? It was Vergil's family name or
    cognomen).

We also know the names of household and sacred instruments, feasts, offerings, priests, etc., such as words meaning 'cup', *cupe,*[79] and *culichna;* 'grave', *śuthi;* 'wine', *vinum;* 'urn', *capra;* sarcophagus', *murs* or *mutana;* 'mirror', *malena, malstria;* 'statue', *flere;* 'incense', *tur* (Lat. *tūs, tūris,* which in turn comes from Greek *thýos*).

We know the words for 'year', *avil;* 'month', *tiur* (this is also the name of the moon goddess written on the bronze liver from Piacenza, see fig. 36); 'day', *tin,* the same word as the name of the sky god, Jupiter, the god of the day (cf. Lat. *deus,* 'god', and *diēs,* 'day', and other Indoeuropean languages; Engl. *Tues-day*).[80]

We also know the words for 'city', **spura,* 'district', *methlum,* and the national name of the Etruscan people, *raśna* (Greek *Rásenna*).

FOREIGN WORDS IN ETRUSCAN

Quite a few foreign words were adopted and more or less transformed: this is of course aside from proper names of gods or heroes, such as Odysseus or Polydeukes (Pollux), already discussed. The Etruscans long took part in the civilization and culture of the peninsula of Italy, and had close contacts with the other neighbouring Italian peoples: the Latins, the Umbrians, the Veneti, the Oscans, and others (map 2). Of course the highest civilization in Italy in the eighth and seventh century B.C. and later was that of the Greeks, and the Etruscans were strongly influenced by their culture. Not only did they adopt the alphabet and the art of writing from Greek, but they also borrowed many outer signs of civilization from the Greeks, as well as the words that went with them. This included Greek mythology, a sign of culture then as it still is today.[81] It also included imported Greek pottery, types of clothing and ways of dressing, and the related vocabulary.[82] Not surprisingly, considering how many vases were imported into Italy from Greece, we recognize a number of names of Greek vases in Etruscan: *qutun*, a handled jug or oinochoe, from the Greek word *kōthōn*; *lechtum* from *lēkythos*, a special Greek pitcher used for rites for the dead; *aska*, an aryballos for oil, from *askós*; *culichna*, a type of handled cup, from Greek *kýlix*.[83] The word *capra*, 'urn', may also have been derived from the Greek *kámptra*, 'box'.[84]

A number of words were borrowed from their Umbrian neighbours to the east: *etera*, the word for 'client' or 'stranger' (Lat. *peregrīnus*); a word for 'basket', *cletram*; more importantly, perhaps, the word for 'city' or 'community', *tuthi* (from the Umbrian word *tota*), and the name of a local god, *crapsti*, perhaps of Umbrian origin.

From Latin come some important words related to religious ritual: *fanu*, 'sacred place', 'sanctuary', from Latin *fānum*; *tura*, 'incense', from *tūs, tūris* (Greek *thýos*); *cupe*, 'cup', from *cuppa*; *Nethuns*, 'Neptune', from *Neptūnus*, and *Selvans*, 'Silvanus'. There is also the word *macstre*, 'master', from the Latin *magister*, and the word *nefts*, for 'grandson', from *nepōs* (cf. 'nephew'). We have seen that the conjunction *-c*, meaning 'and', seems to have been borrowed from Latin *-que*. The chronology of these loan words has to be studied in each case. For Etruscan words in Latin, see p. 60.

CHAPTER VI

ETRUSCAN WRITING: THE AFTERMATH

The Etruscan alphabet spread throughout the whole of Italy and was used for all the languages spoken in the peninsula with the exception of Greek, Messapic, and the native languages of Sicily (maps 2 and 3). The whole of central and northern Italy eventually used alphabets that derived directly from the Etruscan: Umbrian, Oscan, Venetic, Lepontian, Gallic (Gaulish, of north Italy), Picene, Rhaetic, and in part, Latin.

This alphabet spread much farther north as well. Also derived from the Etruscan alphabet by way of the Venetic script were the Germanic runes – the writing used by the Goths (in the Ukraine, Yugoslavia, Rumania, etc.),

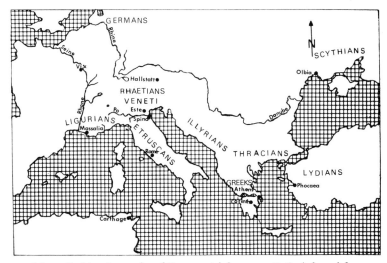

Map 4 Prehistoric peoples of Europe, eighth century B.C. (adapted from *Hallstattkultur*, 1980)

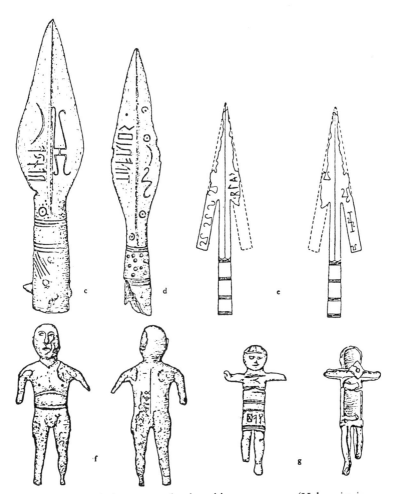

8 Runic inscriptions on spearheads and bronze statuettes (Holmqvist, in
Eggers, *et al., Celtes et Germains,* 1964, 70, fig. 14)

the Germans, the English, the Danes, Norwegians, Swedes, and Icelanders
(map 4).[85] These runes, originally considered to be magic signs, were
carved on weapons or armor to make them more powerful, on other objects
as protection. Several early runes have come down to us carved on
spearheads or helmets (fig. 8). As an example of later runes we can look at
the beautiful ivory casket in the British Museum, the Franks Casket, dating
from the eighth century A.D., whose inscription in runes, running all
around the frame, tells a story about hunting a whale.[86] Most of these runic
inscriptions were incised on stone,[87] and date to a period well within the
Christian era, at a time when Etruscan civilization had long been forgotten.

Yet they testify to the lasting influence of Etruria and its role in bringing civilization, and above all the art of writing, to Europe.

Two questions must be considered concerning the origin of the runes. When were these runes (fig. 9) first adopted from the Etruscan alphabet? And how did this Etruscan influence spread so far north?

Let us take the question of date first. The earliest of these inscriptions date from the first or second century A.D. The first reference to such inscriptions occurs around the same date; the Roman historian Tacitus mentions the runes in his book on Germany, the *Germania*, written in 98 A.D.[88] Yet the runes must have been developed from the Etruscan alphabet long before this time, for the Romans conquered northern Italy around 200 B.C., and thereafter the Teutons or Germanic tribes would have adopted the Latin alphabet, not the Etruscan, which by then belonged to a culture rapidly diminishing in importance. This brings us to the third century B.C. at least, probably much earlier, for the introduction of this writing into Germany. Why is it then that no runes have been found earlier than the first or second century A.D.? The answer is very simple: they were all destroyed. As Tacitus tells us (*Germania* 10.1–3), 'signs' (*notae*) were carved on pieces of wood, particularly beech wood (Latin *fāgus*, 'beech', which corresponds to the English word 'book').[89] Such pieces of wood (*surculī*) would soon rot in a damp northern climate like that of Germany.

The route of this writing can be traced without too much difficulty. A northern Etruscan alphabet was first borrowed, probably from the area of Chiusi,[90] by the Venetic- and Rhaetic-speaking peoples of northern Italy,

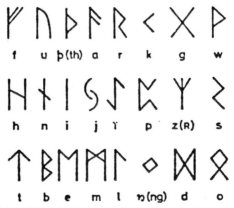

9 Runic alphabet: 'futhark' (From W. Krause, H. Jankuhn, *Die Runenschrift im älteren Futhark*)

and then, across the Alps, by the Germanic tribes of Europe (map 4). Direct contacts between Etruria and Germany go far back in time, to the period of Etruscan supremacy, when everyone flocked to trade with the Etruscan cities and buy some of the mineral wealth they controlled. Northerners imported not only the raw materials, but also the finished bronze work for which the Etruscans were famous throughout the ancient world. Such contacts between Germany and Etruria are confirmed by the German word *Erz*, 'metal', which comes from the name of the Etruscan city of *Arrētium*, Arezzo, famous for its working on metal. The famous Chimaera of Arezzo, discovered during the Renaissance, testifies to the skill of the bronze workers of that Etruscan city (fig. 19).[91]

And when Scipio Africanus asked the Etruscan cities for supplies for his expedition against Hannibal in the second Punic war, Arezzo's principal contribution consisted of arms, weapons and tools.[92] Its flourishing workshops, producing quantities of the shiny red-glazed, relief-decorated Arretine pottery (later imitated in the north as well) continued this tradition of metal-working into the first centuries B.C. and A.D.

Thus, long before Roman merchants reached Germany, Etruscan craftsmen and tradesmen had arrived in these northern regions. They brought with them objects and techniques, and introduced into Europe the invention of writing, and thereby the beginning of the civilization we know.

NOTES

PART TWO

1. Pallottino, *Etruscans* 64–81, with bibliography.
2. Pallottino, *Etruscans* 72–3, 275, pl. 9. See also *infra*, Bibliography: Rix, Brandenstein. M. Gras, in *Mélanges Heurgon* 341–70, esp. 352–6. Grant 57–8.
3. Hesiod, *Theogony* 12, 101ff. Translated by Norman O. Brown (New York, Library of Liberal Arts 1953): 'Circe, the daughter of Hyperion's child, the Sun-god, loved Odysseus, famous for his endurance, and bore Agrius and Latinus, the strong man with no stain. This pair rules over all the famous Tyrsenians in their far-away retreat deep in the sacred islands.' The Lipari islands (also called 'Aeolian' or 'Volcanian') are probably referred to.
4. Herodotus 1, 93–6: 'Apart from the fact that they prostitute their daughters, the Lydian way of life is not unlike our own. The Lydians were the first people we know of to use a gold and silver coinage and to introduce retail trade, and they also claim to have invented the games now commonly played both by themselves and by the Greeks. These games are supposed to have been invented at the time when they sent a colony to settle in Tyrrhenia, and the story is that in the reign of Atys, the son of Manes, the whole of Lydia suffered from a severe famine. For a time the people lingered on as patiently as they could, but later, when there was no improvement, they began to look for something to alleviate their misery. Various expedients were devised: for instance, the invention of dice, knuckle-bones, and ball-games. In fact they claim to have invented all games of this sort except draughts. The way they used these inventions to help them endure their hunger was to eat and play on alternate days – one day playing so continuously that they had no time to think of food, and eating on the next without playing at all. They managed to live like this for eighteen years. There was still no remission of their suffering – indeed it grew worse; so the King divided the population into two groups and determined by drawing lots which should emigrate and which should remain at home. He appointed himself to rule the section whose lot determined that they should remain, and his son Tyrrhenus to command the emigrants. The lots were drawn, and one section went down to the coast at Smyrna, where they built vessels, put aboard all their household effects and sailed in search of a livelihood elsewhere. They passed many countries and finally reached Umbria in the north of Italy, where they settled

and still live to this day. Here they changed their name from Lydians to Tyrrhenians, after the King's son Tyrrhenus, who was their leader.' Translated by A. de Sélincourt, *Herodotus, The Histories*, Penguin Classics (Harmondsworth 1954).

5. Heurgon 98–100.

6. Dionysius of Halicarnassus, *Rom. Ant.* 1.30.1–3. Translated by E. Cary, Loeb Classical Library (1914).

7. Livy, 1.2: 'Etruria, indeed, had at this time both by sea and land filled the whole length of Italy from the Alps to the Sicilian strait with the fame of her name . . .' Cf. Cato (Servius, *ad Aen.* 11.567): *In Tuscorum iure paene omnis Italia fuerat.*

8. *Annals* 11.14.

9. M. Frederiksen, 'The Etruscans in Campania', *IBR* 288.

10. A. Grenier, 'L'alphabet de Marsiliana et les origines de l'écriture à Rome', *Mélanges d'Archéologie et d'Histoire* 41 (1924) 3ff. Pallottino, *Etruscans* 291–2, pl. 93. *Supra*, Chapter I, n. 108.

11. See Chapter I, n. 8. Nestor's cup, found at Ischia in 1954, dates well within the eighth century B.C.

12. Lucretius, *de rerum natura*, 6, 381–2: *non Tyrrhena retro uoluentem carmina frustra/indicia occultae diuum perquirere mentis.* ('Not unwinding Etruscan scrolls from back to front, searching in vain for the gods' hidden will'). Heurgon (278) credits Niebuhr with this explanation of *retro*.

13. The problem of syllabic writing, studied by E. Vetter, F. Slotty, A. Pfiffig, and M. Lejeune, is well summarized by E. Peruzzi, *Mycenaeans in Early Latium* (Rome 1980), Appendix I, 'Mycenaeans and Etruscans', 137–49. In a brilliant analysis of a passage in the work of the Byzantine scholar, Johannes Lydus (sixth century A.D.), dealing with Tarchon, the miraculous child Tages, the *etrusca disciplina*, and the development of a syllabic script in Etruria, Peruzzi convincingly denies any relationship between this Etruscan system and the earlier Mycenean syllabic writing. The Etruscan system 'is not the relic of syllabic-writing habits in an environment which had just gone one step further . . ., but the development of well-mastered alphabetic practices' (Johannes Lydus, *de ostentis* 2.6.B).

14. By 'Italic' we understand, following Devoto and other scholars, Oscan, Umbrian, Marsian, Pelignian and other minor dialects of Central Italy, as distinct from Latin, which we do *not* call Italic.

15. F. Roncalli (*JdI* 95 (1980) 227–64) points out the similarity between the religious ritual text, with its many 'levels', to modern religious texts.

16. See Chapter I, n. 70. For pre-Roman inscriptions in Italy, see G. Bonfante, ed., *Iscrizioni pre-latine (infra*, n. 87). Add to these a new Gaulish–Latin bilingual from Vercelli: M. Lejeune, *CRAI* 1977, 582ff.; M.–G. Tibiletti Bruno, *Rendiconti AccLincei* 31 (1977) 355–76. See also a new Latin inscription, *c.* 500 B.C.: C. Stibbe and others, *Lapis Satricanus* (1980). The Praenestine Fibula has recently been declared a forgery: A. E. Gordon, *The Inscribed Fibula Praenestina*. University of California Publications: Classical Studies 16 (Berkeley, Los Angeles, London

1975); D. Ridgway, 'Manios Faked?', in *Bulletin of the Institute of Classical Studies* 24 (1977) 17–30; M. Guarducci, in *MemLinc* 24 (1980) 415–574.

17. CIE 6213. Source 47.

18. For the Zagreb mummy text, see Roncalli (*supra* n. 15), who presents a convincing reconstruction of the original 'book' from which the wrappings were cut or torn.

19. Pallottino, *Etruscans* 222, 292, pl. 97.

20. Pallottino, *Etruscans* 293, pl. 101.

21. Pallottino, *Etruscans* 221.

22. *TLE* 719. See Chapter I, n. 23.

23. S. Weinstock, 'Martianus Capella and the cosmic system of the Etruscans', *JRS* 36 (1946) 101ff. Pallottino, *Etruscans* 144, 261 n. 15.

24. See Chapter I and Sample Inscriptions.

25. *Supra*, n. 2.

26. Pallottino, *Etruscans* 197–208.

27. The bibliography on the Pyrgi tablets is enormous. See Pallottino, *Etruscans* 90, 93, 221, 249, 255, pls. 12–14. Heurgon, *JRS* 56 (1966) 1ff. presents a good account in English. The results of a seminar held at Tübingen in 1979 on the subject of the goddess to whom the dedication was made have just been published (see Bibliography, *Die Göttin von Pyrgi*). Some scholars still believe, as did Giorgio Levi della Vida, that the Phoenician inscription shows Cypriot features. Others take it as Punic, confirming a Carthaginian presence: Grant 148, 151–5.

28. Vergil, *Aen.* 8.72 etc. *Thybris* is Etruscan. A. Momigliano, 'Thybris Pater', *Rivista di Filologia Classica* 1938, 1–26.

29. Aristotle, *Politics* 3, 9, 1280a, 36.

30. G. Pasquali, 'La grande Roma dei Tarquinii', in *Terze Pagine Stravaganti* (Florence 1942; reprinted 1968) 5–21.

31. Pallottino, *Etruscans* 146, 261–2, pl. 100. According to Pfiffig (279) *frontac* (onomatopoeia) is related to Greek *brontē*, 'thunder', and therefore equivalent to *fulguriator*.

32. *Spitus*: *TLE* 887–9; *Thesaurus, s.v.*

33. Heurgon 83.

34. *Presnt* occurs in several other inscriptions: see *Thesaurus, s.v.*

35. Pallottino, *Etruscans* 201. *TLE* 801–58. G. Bonfante, 'Problemi delle glosse etrusche', *Atti di Grosseto* (Florence 1977) 84. M. Torelli, 'Glosse etrusche: qualche problema di trasmissione', *Mélanges Heurgon* 1001–8.

36. *Atrium*: *TLE* 814. Pallottino, *Etruscans* 176. Walde-Hofmann, Ernout-Meillet, *s.v.* A. Ernout, *Philologica* III (Paris 1965) 30. F. Prayon, *Frühetruskische Grab- und Hausarchitektur* (Heidelberg 1975) 160. *Aisar*: *TLE* 803 (Suet., Dio Cass.). *Verse*: *TLE* 812. *Aclus*: *TLE* 801. Zagreb mummy: Source 54.

37. Torelli, *Mélanges Heurgon*, 1001–8.

38. *TLE* 811. *Arimos* = 'monkey'. Serv. *Aen.* 9.712: *simiae . . . quas Etruscorum lingua arimos dicunt.* Hesychios: *árimos, píthēkos*; cf. Strabo 13.4.6. For monkeys, see D. Rebuffat Emmanuel, *StEtr* 35 (1967) 633–44, and J. Szilágyi, *RA* 1972,

111—26.

39. *Inarime*: Vergil *Aen.* 9.716; Ovid *Met.* 14.89; also Pliny, Lucan, Statius, etc. Cf. Homer, *Iliad* 2.783.

40. *TLE* 843: Servius, *ad Aen.* 2.278; 8.475. Livy 1.34, and Ogilvie 142—3.

41. For *litterae*, see E. Peruzzi, *Origini di Roma* II, 16—24; and *Aspetti culturali del Lazio primitivo* (Florence 1978) 31, 153—4. L. Bonfante. *Etruscan Dress*, 'Appendix II: Vocabulary', 101—4.

42. The word *uīnum* may have come into Etruscan from Latin. It is originally *not* Indoeuropean, and probably came from the Eastern Mediterranean area (Georgia): G. Bonfante, 'Das Problem des Weines und die linguistische Paläontologie', *Antiquitates Indogermanicae. Gedenkschrift für H. Günter* (Innsbruck 1974) 85—90; and *Out of Etruria* 10. For the history of the interpretation of Etruscan, see Pallottino, *Etruscans* 189—208.

43. Laris Pulenas: Pallottino, *Etruscans* 200, 219. Grant 126. (Chapter I, n. 33). F. Coarelli, 'Il sepolcro degli Scipioni', *DdA* 6 (1972) 36—105. Iguvine tablets: Pallottino, *Etruscans* 223.

44. See chart of alphabet and transcription. Linguists classify consonants as follows, according to (1) the place where they are articulated in the mouth, and (2) the way they are articulated. (The sounds are those of English.) Velars: *k, g, n* (as in *think*). Dentals: *t, d, n.* Bilabials: *p, b, m, w.* Labiodentals: *f, v.* Interdentals: *th* (as in *think*), and *th* (as in *this*). Stops: *k, t, p, g, d, b.* Voiceless stops: *k, t, p, ch.* Voiced stops: *g, d, b, j.* Fricatives: *f, v, th* (*think, this*). Voiceless fricatives: *f, th* (*think*), *s.* Voiced fricatives: *v, z, th* (*this*). Aspirates: *k, t, p* in initial position. Semiconsonants: *y* (*yes*), *u* (*quick*).

45. Pallottino, *Etruscans* 210, 270.

46. *K* stands for *Kalendae*, from which comes the word 'calendar'.

47. *C* stands for *Caius*, pronounced *Gaius*. The same sign was also pronounced as a *k*, as in *Kaiser* (from *Caesar*).

48. The sign here transcribed as *v* always had a bilabial pronunciation, like English *w*. Latin *u* had two similar values: as a vowel in *bucca*, and as a semivowel in *uīnum, uenit, uincit, nāuis.* The Latins were thus free to use the Greek *digamma*, F, to represent the sound of our *f*, while the Etruscans could not, because they needed F for the *w* sound. In Etruscan, as in Latin, *f* was probably bilabial, like *w, p,* and *b,* and not labiodental, as is English *f.* Latin inscriptions often have *m* before *f*, like *imferi* for *inferi.*

49. Pallottino, *Etruscans* 210. The two sibilants Ϻ and S, corresponding respectively to the Phoenician letters *sade* and *šin*, are transcribed as *ś* and *s*. (For the transcription of the other signs for *s*, see *TLE* p. 13; Pfiffig 20.) In the north Etruscan cities, Ϻ is regularly used to indicate the genitive ending (see *infra*, n. 65). In the new inscription of the *Clautie* family, *CIE* 6213 (source 47), ⟨ and ⟩ are used for the sibilants. The use of a variety of signs may of course simply betray the survival of earlier forms of spelling (*i.e.* 'historical spelling' as in English), or of conventional signs (like the special form of German double *ss*): G. Bonfante, *AGI* 56 (1971) 168. The distinction was considered to be important by the Etruscans themselves.

Cristofani (*IBR* 380) suggests that the sound [*s*] was represented by *sade*, [*ss*] by the three-stroke *sigma*; but see G. Bonfante, *AGI* 61 (1976) 269; 272. There seems to have been some confusion between *s* and *ś*, often used without distinction in the same place, with the same function. Yet there is reason to believe that *s* was pronounced as a dental fricative (English *same*), while *ś* represented a palatal fricative (English *shame*); for *husiur*, 'children', was also written *huśur* (*husiur* must have become *husyur and then *huśur*, with palatal *ś*). The form *husiur* is likely to be the older, since it is found near Perugia, in a peripheral and therefore more conservative area.

50. For *p* and *t* we have no examples, perhaps because none has yet been found.

51. C. de Simone, *StEtr* 37 (1970) 115–39. M. Cristofani, *AGI* 56 (1971) 40, n. 9; *StEtr* 41 (1973) 181ff.; *Introduzione* 78, 83.

52. Contrast Italian *ceppo* ('log', 'branch') and *zeppo* ('full to the brim'), where the words have different meanings, with *rinuncia: rinunzia* ('he renounces'), *annuncia: annunzia* ('he announces'), or *pronuncia, pronunzia* ('he pronounces'), where the *z* and *c* represent only phonetic variants. The conclusion is important: the phonetic or phonemic value of a phoneme depends on its position in the word. G. Bonfante, *AGI* 61 (1976) 272.

53. Pliny *apud* Priscian II.26.16: '*o* aliquot Italiae gentes non habebant, sed loco eius ponebant *u*, et maxime Umbri et Tusci'. Pfiffig 29.

54. De Simone (*L'etrusco arcaico* 72) thinks that in *Atmite* (from Greek *Ádmētos*) and in *Catmite* (from *Gadymēdēs* instead of *Ganymēdēs*) the *i*, corresponding to Greek *ē*, was preserved because the Etruscans also pronounced it as a long vowel. Even if he were right, these words, of foreign origin, constitute insufficient evidence for the existence of these long vowels in Etruscan. Every language treats certain foreign words in a special way.

55. Cristofani 47. *Faustus* > *Fasti*; *Raufe* > *Rafe* (Latin *Rūfus*, from early Latin *Roufos).

56. The letter *a* is often not dropped because the sound *ă* is by its nature slightly longer than *ĕ*, *ĭ* or *ŭ*. See for example Latin *cápio: óccupo, ágō: éx-ĭgo, alter: ad-ulter*, in which *ă* becomes *ŭ* or *ĭ*. *Amake* in Etruscan becomes first *amuce*, then *amce*.

57. See *infra*, n. 78.

58. Our use of the Latin terms *nominative, genitive, dative*, etc. for Etruscan is obviously an approximation. Neither in Latin nor Etruscan does the genitive (or dative, or accusative) correspond exactly to the Greek or to the German cases. Doubtful cases such as the *modalis*, the *adlative*, the *ablative*, will not be listed. Following Pfiffig (78) we call 'definite accusative' a form which is certainly an accusative, but has an ending -*ni* or -*i*, which the 'usual' accusative (identical with the nominative) does not have. Scholars have up to now failed to discover any difference in function between the two accusatives. The genitive has frequently the function that we attribute to the dative: e.g., *Venel Atelinas gave this to* 'the sons of Jupiter' (*TLE* 156), where 'sons of Jupiter' is in the genitive.

59. The word *clan*, 'son', very frequent on tombs, shows a mysterious change in

the vowel: *clan: clenśi: clenar*. We can offer no explanation for this strange fact, which is however absolutely certain.

60. Here and elsewhere in the book, an asterisk is used to indicate a word whose existence can be deduced from other evidence, though it does not appear in any text.

61. *s* and *ś* frequently alternate without any clear reasons; but see *infra*, n. 65.

62. Looking at the paradigm of e.g. **śpura* or *methlum*, one is at first tempted to consider Etruscan a kind of agglutinative language since to the nominative singular *methlum*, genitive *methlum-es*, locative *methlumth(i)*, etc., are opposed the nominative plural *methlumer*, genitive *methlum-er-s*, definite accusative *methlum-er-i*. We observe that the endings of the plural are the same as those of the singular; but in the plural, between the stem and the endings, the (pluralizing) element *-er-* is added. The same happens, however, also in purely 'inflectional' languages: German singular *das Kind, dem Kinde* (dative); plural *die Kinder, den Kindern*.

63. See M. Cristofani, 'L'indicazione dell' 'età' in etrusco', *AGI* 58 (1973) 157–64; 'Recent advances', in *IBR*, 400.

64. Sometimes the genitive form is ambiguous. Scholars argue about the gender of the person buried in the Regolini-Galassi tomb, whose silverware is dedicated, *larthial*. Chapter I, nn. 51, 53. (No. 5, fig. 12.)

65. Typical of north Etruria is the spelling of the genitive ending in *s* with a *ś* (*M*). Roncalli, on the Zagreb mummy wrappings, *JdI* 95 (1980) 252, M. Durante, in *Studi linguistici in onore di V. Pisani* I (Brescia 1969) 299. H. Rix, *Das etruskische Cognomen* (Wiesbaden 1963). C. de Simone, 'Fremde Gentilnamen in Etrurien in archaischer Zeit', *Aufnahme* (1981) 89–93. This 'gentilizio', as it is called in Italian, has been the object of several recent studies: see *infra*, Bibliography.

66. G. Körte, *JdI* 12 (1897) 57–80. F. Messerschmidt, A. von Gerkan, *Nekropolen von Vulci. JdI. Ergänzungsheft* 12 (1930) 62–163. T. Dohrn, in Helbig⁴, 204–17, No. 3239. L. Bonfante, *AJAH* 3 (1978) [1980] 136–62, with recent bibliography.

67. On the numerals on the 'Tuscania' dice, see Pfiffig, 123–30; and Cristofani, *IBR* 407–8, with preceding bibliography. The 'Tuscania' dice do *not* come from Tuscania: Colonna, *StEtr* 46 (1978) 115. *cezp* is believed to be *8* because of the gloss *chosfer* = October: *TLE* 838. For declension of numerals, see Pfiffig, 126. On the numerals 'one' to 'six', see A. Torp, *Etruskische Beiträge* I (1902–3) 64ff., 100ff. The theory that *mach* = 1 is impossible because, in the inscription *huśur mach acnanas* (*TLE* 887), 'he had *mach* children', *huśur* is a plural form, so *mach* cannot mean 'one' in the singular.

68. Epigram, *Anthologia Palatina*, 14.8.

69. M. Lejeune, *BSL* 76 (1981) 241ff.

70. Pfiffig 34, 38, 289.

71. C. de Simone, *StEtr* 38 (1970) 115–39. Cristofani, *IBR* 397–8.

72. C. de Simone, *Le ricerche* (Florence 1973) 108.

73. An 'opposition' of *-ce* and *-che* exists only in this position. See *supra*, n. 51–2.

74. The ending *-che* is phonemically distinct from *-ce* and indicates a passive: *mi*

titasi cver menache = 'I was given as a gift to Tita'. There is almost general agreement about the passive value of *-che*. There is some discussion about the form *Tita-si*. It is very likely a dative, as we have translated. But another possible translation is: 'I was given as a gift by Tita', that is, *Titasi* would be an agent. It is of course possible that the dative was used for the agent, as sometimes happens in Latin with the participles. The same holds true for the other examples of passive we examine below (*mi* is certainly a nominative). See Cristofani, *IBR* 397–8; de Simone, *StEtr* 38 (1970) 128ff.

75. For *avil* and *avils* see *supra*, n. 63.

76. Cristofani, *Introduzione*, 66–7, 74, 88, 159. G. Bonfante, *AGI* 61 (1976) 273.

77. '*Muluvanice* can be used in both sacred and profane contexts, while *turuce* can only express the concept of sacred dedication. *Menace* and *zinace* can be related to pottery activities.' Cristofani, *IBR* 406–7; cf. Colonna, *RM* 82 (1975) 181–92.

78. E. Fiesel, *Namen des griechischen Mythos im Etruskischen* (1928); C. de Simone, *Die griechischen Entlehnungen im Etruskischen* (1968–70). See also H. Rix, 'Das Eindringen griechischer Mythen in Etrurien nach Aussage der mythologis-chen Namen', *Aufnahme* (1981) 96–106.

79. From which comes Latin *cupa*, Italian *coppa*, French *coupe*, English *cup*.

80. On the religious, ritual character and context of this vocabulary, see *supra*, Chapter III, section on Glosses.

81. Pfiffig, *Religio Etrusca*; and review by E. Simon, *Göttingische Gelehrte Anzeigen* 232 (1980) 204.

82. L. Bonfante, *Etruscan Dress*, 81–104.

83. *TLE* 63, 762, etc. Cristofani, *IBR* 406–7, with bibliography. G. Colonna, 'Nomi etruschi di vasi', *Arch. Class.* 25–6 (1973–4) 132–50. *Thina* (Caere) from Greek *dínos*, understood as *olla*, recalls the *tina* of Varro's account of symposia. Through Etruscan, Greek *dínos* came into Latin as *tina* (whence Italian *tino*, 'vat').

84. *Capra*: Paul. Festus 48. F.-H. Pairault Massa, in *Caratteri dell'ellenismo nelle urne etrusche* (1978) 155, 164.

85. For the origin of the runes, see G. Bonfante, 'Arezzo e gli Etruschi', in *Out of Etruria* (1981) 124–34, with bibliography.

86. The casket has been in the British Museum since 1867; the right side is in the Museo Nazionale, Florence. T. D. Kendrick, *Anglo-Saxon Art*, London, 1938, pl. XLV, i, and J. Beckwith, *Ivory Carvings in Early Medieval England*, London, 1972, fig. 4. On the mythological representation of Wayland the Smith, see K. Crocker, 'The lame smith', *ArchNews* 6 (1977) 67–71.

87. The Germanic people learned to write on stone from the Romans: G. Bonfante, in *Le iscrizioni pre-latine in Italia. Atti dei Convegni Lincei* 39. *Accademia Nazionale dei Lincei* (Rome 1979) 223. Cf. also A. Tovar, *Zeitschrift für Celtische Philologie* 34 (1975) 14.

88. Tacitus, *Germania* 10, 1–2: *Sortium consuetudo simplex: uirgam frugiferae arbori decisam in surculos amputant eosque notis quibusdam discretos super candidam uestem temere ac fortuito spargunt.* '. . . the method of drawing lots is the same among them all. A

branch is cut from a fruit-bearing tree and split up into slips; these are distinguished by certain signs and spread casually and at random over a white cloth'. (Translation adapted from W. Peterson, *Tacitus. Dialogus, Agricola, Germania*, Loeb Classical Library, Cambridge, Mass. 1914).

89. All these derive from an Indoeuropean word. Cf. German *Buch-stabe*, 'letter', Latin *fagus*, German *Buch*, English *book*: Klein, *Etymological Dictionary*, s.v. G. Bonfante, in *Out of Etruria* 128–9.

90. G. Bonfante, in *Out of Etruria* 133. M. Cristofani, map of the distribution of the Etruscan alphabet in Italy, in *Pop. e Civ.* fig. 6; *ibid. IBR* 385, fig. 2; *ibid. ANRW* 1, 2 (1972) 482.

91. Chapter I, nn. 120–2.

92. Livy 28.45.

PART THREE

STUDY AIDS

SOURCES
(Sample inscriptions and texts)

1. Alphabet on a miniature (88 × 51 mm) ivory writing tablet from Marsiliana d'Albegna, *c*. 650 B.C. A model Etruscan alphabet of twenty-six letters is engraved on one side. The back of this ornament, probably worn at the neck, was originally covered with gold leaf. Florence, Mus. Arch. (Pallottino, *Etruscans* pl. 93) (figs. 10a, 11).

10 Etruscan model alphabets, 650–600 B.C.
(*a*) Marsiliana d'Albegna, ivory tablet (cf. fig. 11)
(*b*) Cerveteri, Regolini-Galassi tomb, bucchero vase (*TLE* 55) (cf. fig. 12)
(*c*) Viterbo, bucchero vase in the shape of a rooster (cf. fig. 13)
(*d*) Formello, Veii, bucchero amphora (*TLE* 49) (source 4)

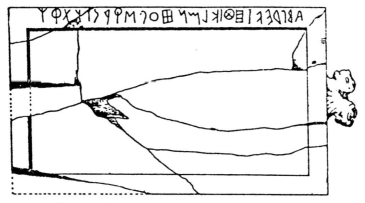

11 Ivory tablet from Marsiliana d'Albegna with model alphabet. 8.8 cm × 5 cm. Florence, Museo Archeologico. (source 1).

2. Bucchero flask from the Regolini-Galassi tomb at Cerveteri, *c.* 650 B.C. (*TLE* 55) (fig. 12) Syllabary and alphabet:

> *ci ca cu ce vi va vu ve*
> *zi za zu ze hi ha hu he*
> *thi tha thu the mi ma mu me n*
> *ni na nu ne pi pa pu pe ri ra ru re*
> *si sa su se chi cha chu che gi ga gu ge ti ta tu te*
> *a b d e v z h th i k [l m n] ś o p ś r s t u ś ph ch*

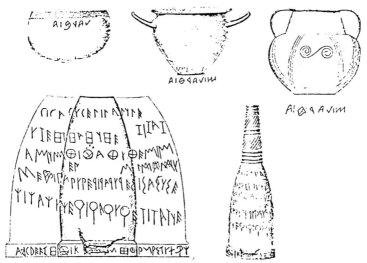

12 Alphabet, syllabary, and inscriptions on objects from the Regolini-Galassi tomb. Caere, Vatican, Museo Etrusco Gregoriano. (sources 2 and 5)

3. Bucchero vase or inkwell in the shape of a rooster, incized with the Etruscan alphabet, from Viterbo *c.* 600 B.C. (fig. 13). New York, Metropolitan Museum.

13 (a–c) Bucchero vase or inkwell in the shape of a rooster. (The Metropolitan Museum of Art, Fletcher Fund, 1924) (source 3)

4. The 'Formello Alphabet', incised around the neck of an Archaic bucchero amphora from Veii, *c.* 650 B.C. (*TLE* 49) (fig. 10d). Rome, Villa Giulia Museum.

5. Silver cup and amphoriskos from the Regolini-Galassi tomb at Cerveteri, *c.* 650 B.C. (*TLE* 54) (fig. 12):

mi larthia
'I (belong to) Larth' (or 'Larthi', a woman)

6. Two oinochoai from Cerveteri, *c.* 675 B.C. (*TLE* 63):

mi qutun karkanaś
'I (am) the pitcher of Karkana'

(Cf. Greek *kōthōn*, 'pitcher').

7. Impasto oinochoe or pitcher from Narce, seventh century B.C. (*TLE* 28):

mi qutun lemausnaś
'I (am) the pitcher of Lemausna'

(Cf. Faliscan (archaic Latin dialect): *eco quto euotenosio*, 'I am the pitcher of Euotenos': Staccioli 58)

8. Bucchero aryballos, provenance unknown, *c.* 600 B.C. (*TLE* 762).
Monte Carlo, Musée Charles Albert:

> *mlakas se la aska mi eleivana*
> '(He) has offered (me) to Silvanus, a jar I am for unguents'
> ('I am the unguent-bottle that was given to the god Silvanus')

(Cf. the Greek words *askós*, 'bottle', and *élaiwon*, 'oil', or 'unguent'. Poupé, *Etudes Etrusco-Italiques*, 245, No. 32, pl. 25, 3; de Simone I, 27; Maggiani, *SE* 40 (1972) 183–7.)

9. Bucchero amphora from Cerveteri, *c.* 600 B.C. (*TLE* 868):

> *mi aranth ramuthaśi veśtiricinala muluvanice*
> 'Me Arnth to Ramtha Vestirikina dedicated'
> ('Arnth dedicated me to Ramtha Vestirikina')

(*mi* is a mistake for *mini*, accusative).

10. Stele representing a warrior armed with crested helmet and round shield, brandishing a double axe, from Vetulonia, *c.* 600 B.C. (*TLE* 363; Vetter, *SE* 24 (1955–6) 301–10) (fig. 14):

> *(a) veleś feluskeś tuśnutn(ie) panalaś mini muluvaneke hirumina phersnachs*
> 'To Aulus Feluske, glory! (. . . *panalaś*?) Me dedicated Hirumina from Perusia'
> ('To Aulus Feluske, glory! Herminius from Perugia dedicated me')

(This is the earliest use of the new Etruscan letter 8 for the sound 'f'. For *phersnachs*, 'from Perusia', see No. 43.)

14 Stele of Avele Feluske, from Vetulonia

(source 10)

15 Stele of Avile Tite, from Volterra (source 11)

11. Funerary stone stele from Volterra, representing a male figure armed with lance and knife, wearing shoulder-length hair and short chiton, *c.* 530 B.C. (*TLE* 386; *ED* 68) (fig. 15). Volterra, Museo Guarnacci:

mi aviles tites . . . uchsie mulenike
'I (belong to) Aulus Tite . . . Uchsie dedicated (me)'

16 Stele of Larth Tharnie, from Pomarance
(Volterra) (source 12)

12. Funerary stone stele from Pomarance, near Volterra, with representation of a male figure with long hair, three-quarter-length chiton and
pointed shoes, holding a large knife in the right hand, 550–540 B.C. (*TLE*
407) (fig. 16). Florence, Mus. Arch.:

mi larthia tharnies . . . uchulni muluvuneke
'I (belong to) Larth Tharnie . . . Uchulni dedicated (me).'

13. Funerary stone stele from Fiesole with representation of a male figure
wearing long hair in the Ionic style and a *perizoma*, holding a spear and an
axe. H. 1.38 m. *c.* 525 B.C. (*CIE* 1; *ED* fig. 33). (fig. 17). Florence, Casa
Buonarroti.

mi larthi aninies
'I (belong to) Larth Aninie' or
mi larthia ninies
'I (belong to) Larth Ninie'

17 Stele of Larth Ninie, from Fiesole.
(source 13)

14. Bucchero amphora from Cerveteri, *c*. 600 B.C. (*TLE* 57):

> *mini mulvanice mamarce velchanaś*
> 'me dedicated Mamarce Velchana'
> ('Mamarce Velchana dedicated me')

15. Votive inscription on a bucchero vase from the Portonaccio temple at Veii, *c*. 550 B.C. (*TLE* 35):

> *mini muluv(an)ece avile vipiiennas*
> 'Aulus Vipiiennas dedicated me'

(Proves that Aulus and Caelius Vibenna could have been real people and not mythical figures. The date, mid-sixth century B.C., according to Roman tradition, is that of Servius Tullius, king of Rome (Cristofani, *IBR* 397; Pallottino, *IBR* 216, 219. J. Heurgon, *Mélanges Carcopino*, Rome 1976, 521).)

16. On a plate from the sanctuary at Pyrgi, *c.* 500 B.C. (*TLE* 877):

unial
'(I belong to) Uni'

17. On the architrave of a chamber tomb in the necropolis of Crocifisso del Tufo at Orvieto. *c.* 550–500 B.C. (*TLE* 242):

mi mamarces velthienas
'I (am the grave) of Mamarce Velthiena'

18. On a red-figure Attic kylix from Tarquinia, attributed to Oltos, *c.* 500 B.C. (*TLE* 156; Cristofani 138):

itun turuce venel atelinas tinas cliniiaras
'This dedicated Venel Atelina to the sons of Tinia'
('Venel Atelina dedicated this to the sons of Tinia', i.e. 'the Dioskouroi, Castor and Pollux.')

19. 'Amazon sarcophagus', from a tomb at Tarquinia, fourth century B.C. (*TLE* 123):

ramtha zertnai thui cesu
'Ramtha Zertna here lies'
('Ramtha Zertna lies here')

20. Crater from Vulci with red-figure decoration representing Alcestis (*alcsti*) offering her life for her husband, Admetus (*atmite*), flanked by two demons, second half of fourth century B.C. (*TLE* 334; Beazley *EVP* 133; de Simone 15, 29, 37; Slotty, *SE* 19 (1946–47) 243) (fig. 18). Paris,

18 Red-figure crater from Vulci with the farewell of Alcestis and Admetus
(source 20)

19 Chimaera of Arezzo (source 22)

Bibliothèque Nationale:

> *atmite. alcsti.*
> 'Admetus'. 'Alcestis'.
> *eca: ersce: nac: achrum: flerthrce*
> 'She went thus to Acheron (and) sacrificed herself'

21. Inscription on wall in the Tomba dell'Orco, Tarquinia. Fourth century B.C. (*TLE* 87. Torelli, *ET*).

> ... *churinas an zilath amce mechl rasnal* ...
> *purth ziiace* [read *zilace*] ...
> *ravnthu* (...) *thefrinai* (...) *ati nacnuva*
> 'Churinas (family name) he was *zilath* (praetor) of the people of Etruria ...
> (he) governed as *purth* (dictator?) ... Ravnthu Thefrinai, the grandmother (erected this).'

22. Bronze statue of the Chimaera, from Arezzo. Inscribed on front right leg, early fourth century B.C. (*TLE* 643) (fig. 19).

> *tinścvil*
> 'Offering belonging to Tinia'

23. Stone cippus from Cortona (*TLE* 632):

tular raśnal
'Boundaries of the Etruscan people'

24. Funerary inscription of a man's sarcophagus from Tarquinia, end of fourth century B.C. (*TLE* 128; Staccioli 96):

partunus vel velthurus śatlnalc ramthas
'Vel Partunus, of Velthur and of Satlnei Ramtha
clan avils lupu XXIIX
the son, of years (was) dead (at) 28'
('Vel Partunus, son of Velthur and of Satlnei Ramtha, (was) dead (when he
was) 28 years old).'

25. Funerary inscription of a man's sarcophagus from Tarquinia (Sarcofago del Magnate), fourth or third century B.C. (*TLE* 126):

velthur partunus larisaliśa clan ramthas
'Velthur Partunus, son of the son of Laris, son of Ramtha Cuclni, praetor of
cuclnial zilch cechaneri tenthas avil svalthas LXXXII
sacred functions (he) served; years he lived 82'.
('Velthur Partunus, grandson of Laris and son of Ramtha of Cuclnia, served as
magistrate in charge of sacred functions [cf. Latin *praetor*]. He lived for eighty-
two years'.)

26. An engraved mirror from Volterra, representing Juno (*Uni*)
suckling Herakles (*Hercle*) in order to make him immortal, in an Italic
variant of the myth. Hera (*Uni*) thus adopts Herakles, in the solemn
presence of gods who serve as witnesses. The inscription explains the scene,
and calls Herakles the 'son of Juno' (*Uni-al clan*). *c.* 300 B.C. (*TLE* 399;
ES 5. 60) (fig. 20):

eca: sren: tva: ichnac: hercle: unial: clan: thra: sce
('This image shows how Herakles, the son of Uni, suckled [milk]')

(*tva* must be a third person singular of a verb; *thrasce*, the third person
singular past perfect.)

20 Mirror from Volterra, showing Uni nursing Hercle (source 26)

21 Mirror with Turan and Atunis (Adonis) (source 27)

27. Bronze mirror with engraved decoration: Venus (*Turan*) and Adonis, a seated attendant, and Minerva. Inscribed on Minerva's shield, *c.* 300 B.C. (*TLE* 752; *ED* 83) (fig. 21):

tite cale: atial: turce malstria: cver
'Titus Calus to his mother gave (this) mirror as a gift'
('Titus Calus gave (this) mirror to his mother as a gift')

22 Mirror with Leda's family and the egg (source 28)

28. Bronze mirror with engraved decoration from Porano (Volsinii). Perugia, Mus. Civ. Third century B.C. (*TLE* 219; Beazley, *JHS* 69 (1949) 15, fig. 20; de Simone, I, 106.7.) (fig. 22). *Castur* hands the egg from which Helen is to be born to his father Tyndareus (*Tuntle*), in the presence of his mother Leda (*Latva*), his brother Pollux or Polydeukes (*Pultuce*), and Venus (*Turan*). On the border is an additional inscription, incised when the mirror was put in the tomb:

ceithurneal śuthina
('grave offering of Ceithurna')

23 Mirror with Orestes' matricide (source 29)

29. Bronze mirror with engraved decoration. Orestes (*Urusthe*) killing
Clytemnestra (*Cluthumustha*), while *Nathum*, probably a Fury, brandishing
two snakes, looks on. Below, in the exergue, Jason (*Heiasum*) slays a dragon.
From Veii, fourth century B.C. (*ES* 238; de Simone, I, 45.3) (fig. 23).
Berlin, Antiquarium.

24 Mirror with Perseus and Medusa (source 30)

30. Bronze mirror with engraved decoration. Perseus (*Pherse*), with Minerva (*Menrva*) seated behind him, prepares to behead the sleeping Medusa (*Metus*). From Chiusi, third century B.C. (*ES* 5, 67; de Simone I, 94; *ED* 148) (fig. 24).

25 Mirror with Atropos (Athrpa) (source 31)

31. Bronze mirror with engraved decoration. Atropos (*Athrpa*) ham-
mers the nail of Fate in the presence of the two pairs of lovers, Atalanta and
Meleager (*Atlenta, Meliacr*), and Venus and Adonis (*Turan, Atunis*), *c.* 320
B.C. (Beazley, *JHS* 69 (1949) 12, fig. 15; Herbig, *Götter und Dämonen*², pl.
7; de Simone, I 90). (fig. 25). Berlin, Antiquarium.

26 Mirror with Semele and Fufluns (source 32)

32. Bronze mirror with engraved decoration. Semele (*Semla*) embraces her son Bacchus (*Fufluns*) in the presence of Apollo (*Apulu*). From Vulci, fourth century B.C. (*ES* 1, 83; Beazley, *JHS* 69 (1949) 6, pl. 6A, fig. 7; de Simone I, 110, pl.9, fig. 13). (fig. 26). Berlin, Antiquarium.

27 Mirror with Tinia giving birth to Menrva (source 33)

33. Bronze mirror with engraved decoration. Zeus (*Tinia*) gives birth to
Menerva, assisted by two attendants, *Thanr* and *Ethauśva*. From Palestrina
(Praeneste), fourth century B.C. (*ES* 5, pl. 6; BM 67) (fig. 27). London,
British Museum.

28 Mirror with Lasa holding a scroll (source 34)

34. Bronze mirror with engraved decoration. To the left, a seated male figure, Amphiaraos (*Hamphiare*); to the right, Ajax (*Aivas*). In the centre, a winged, female figure unrolls a scroll on which are written the characters' names: *Lasa, Aivas, Hamphiare* (Pfiffig, *Religio Etrusca*, fig. 10) (fig. 28). London, British Museum.

29 Mirror with Cacu and the Vibenna brothers (source 35)

35. Engraved bronze mirror from Bolsena. *Cacu*, playing the lyre, and *Artile*, reading an open diptych on his knees, are ambushed by the Vibenna brothers, Aulus and Caelius (*Aule Vipinas, Caile Vipinas*), third century B.C. (*ES* 5.127; BM 633; Beazley, *JHS* 69 (1949), 16–17, fig. 22; Brendel 415) (fig. 29). London, British Museum.

30 Votive statue of a *haruspex* (source 36)   *31* Votive statue of Apollo (source 37)

36. Bronze votive statuette of *haruspex*, provenance unknown, fourth century B.C. (*TLE* 736; *ED* 137) (fig. 30). Vatican, Museo Etrusco Gregoriano:

> *tn turce vel sveitus*
> 'This gave Vel Sveitus'
> ('Vel Sveitus gave this')

37. Bronze votive statuette of a young man (Apollo?), wearing laurel wreath, jewelry, and boots: 26 cm (*TLE* 737; Pfiffig, *Religio Etrusca*, fig. 110). (fig. 31). Paris, Bibliothèque Nationale:

> *mi fleres spulare aritimi fasti ruifris t(u)rce clen cecha*
> 'I (am) the statue (or votive offering) to Spulare Artemis (which) Fasti (wife)
> of Ruifri gave on behalf of her son, rightly (*iure merito*)'
> ('I am the statue, or votive offering (which) Fasti, wife of Ruifri, gave according
> to ritual to Artemis Spulare (?) on behalf of her son'.)

38. Bronze votive statuette of double-faced divinity, from Cortona, fourth or third century B.C. (*TLE* 640):

v. cvinti arntiaś. culśanśl. alpan. turce.
'V(elia) Quintia, (the daughter) of Arnth, to Culsans willingly gave.'
('Velia Quintia, the daughter of Arnth, willingly gave this to Culsans.')

A similar statuette was dedicated to the god Selvans, probably Silvanus (*TLE* 641). (See Pfiffig, *Religio Etrusca* 246, fig. 108) (fig. 32).

39. Identical inscription incised on the front of five bronze statuettes, male and female, from a sanctuary near Lake Trasimeno. Fifth century B.C. (*TLE* 625, corrected by Colonna, *Riv. Stor. Ant.* 6–7 [1976–77] 45–67).

mi celś atial celthi
'I (belong to, have been given to) Cel the mother, here (in this sanctuary)'.

(The genitive ending written with an *ś* is typical of north Etruria. *Celthi* is the locative of the demonstrative pronoun *ca: clthi, calthi*, in an older variant (cf. *TLE* 135, *calti śuthiti*). The inscription mentions only the god to whom the gift is dedicated; archaic monuments gave the name of the person giving the gift. *Cel* is a mother goddess: her son, Celsclan, appears on a mirror of the fifth century, *TLE* 368. *Cel* appears on the Piacenza liver.) (Source 49, fig. 36).

40. Sarcophagus of a man from Tarquinia (*TLE* 129):

velthur larisal clan cuclnial thanchvilus lupu avils XXV
'Velthur of Laris son (and) of Cuclni Tanaquil (was) dead years twenty-five'
('Velthur, son of Lars and of Tanaquil Cuclni, died at twenty-five years')

41. Wall painting from the Tomba Querciola II, Tarquinia. Arnth is accompanied by a Charun to the Gates of the Underworld, where his father (also accompanied by a Charun) greets him. Third century B.C. (*CIE* 5493; Pfiffig, *Religio Etrusca*, fig. 97) (fig. 33):

anes arnth velthuru(s) clan lupu avils ↑
'Anes Arnth, son of Velthur, (was) dead at the age of fifty'

(↑ is the Etruscan symbol for '50').

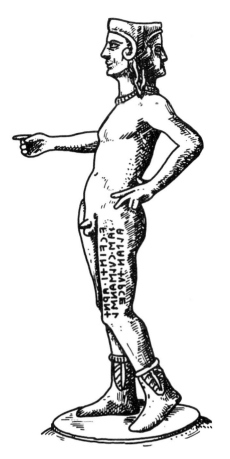

32 Votive statuette of a double-faced divinity (source 38)

33 Wall painting from the Tomba della Querciola (source 41)

34 Wall painting from the Tomb of Orcus (source 42)

42. Wall painting from the Tomba dell'Orco, Tarquinia. The Greek Underworld, with the ghosts of Agamemnon (. . . *memrun*, that is, *achmemrun*) and Teiresias (*hinthial teriasals*). Fourth century B.C. (*TLE* 88). (*Hinthial* means 'shadow', 'ghost', 'reflection in a mirror', Lat. *umbra*). (Fig. 34).

43. Painted decoration on the walls of the François tomb at Vulci, belonging to the Saties family. The tomb construction dates from the fifth century B.C., the elaborate decorative programme from the fourth. In each of the three groups or cycles of decoration, painted inscriptions identify the individual figures (F. Messerschmidt, *Nekropole von Vulci, JdI* Ergänzung-sheft, Berlin, 1930. T. Dohrn, in Helbig⁴, No. 3239. *TLE* 293–303. *CIE* 5247–81).

Names of members of the family and mythological characters
Family:
    vel saties. arnza
'Vel Saties'. 'little Arnth'

thanchvil verati helś atrś (*TLE* 301; *CIE* 5278)
'Tanaquil Verati, her own grave'

tarnai thana satial sec (*TLE* 302; *CIE* 5285).
'Tarna Thana, of Sati the daughter'

ravnthu seitithi. ativu sacniśa aturś. (*TLE* 303; *CIE* 5247: grave cippus in entrance)
'Ravnthu Seitithi (lies here). Her mother dedicated the grave'.

Mythological figures:
   aivas. caśntra. Ajax and Cassandra (*CIE* 5248–5249)
   phuinis. nestur. Phoenix and Nestor (*CIE* 5251–5252)
   evzicle (?) *(pul)nice.* Eteocles and Polyneices (*CIE* 5254–5255)
   sisphe. amphare. Sisyphos and Amphiaraos (*CIE* 5280–5281)

Battle scene:
   Larth Ulthes (Lars Voltius) is killing *Laris Papathnas Velznach* (Lars Papatius, or Fabatius, of Volsinii). *Rasce* (Rascius) is killing *Pesna Arcmsnas Sveamach* (Pesna Arcmsnas from Sovana). *Aule Vipinas* (Aulus Vibenna) is killing an adversary whose name (*Venthica . . . plsachs*) is mutilated, but suggests a man from Falerii.
   Marce Camitlnas (Marcus Camitlnas) kills *Cneve Tarchunies Rumach* (Cnaeus Tarquinius of Rome).
   Finally, *Macstrna* (Mastarna) cuts the bonds of *Caile Vipinas* (Caelius Vibenna) (*TLE* 297–300; *CIE* 5266–73).

Sacrifice of the Trojan Prisoners:
   Achle (Achilles) slits the throat of a Trojan prisoner (*Truials*) in the presence of *Achmemrun* (Agamemnon), the ghost of Patrocles (*hinthial Patrucles*), *Vanth, Charu(n)* (Charon) and the two Ajaxes, Ajax the son of Oileus (*Aivas Vilatas*) and Ajax son of Telamon (*Aivas Tlamunus*), each of whom brings on another Trojan prisoner (*Truials*) (*CIE* 5256–65) (fig. 35).

_____

Overleaf
35 Wall painting from the François Tomb. Sacrifice of the Trojan prisoners
(source 43)

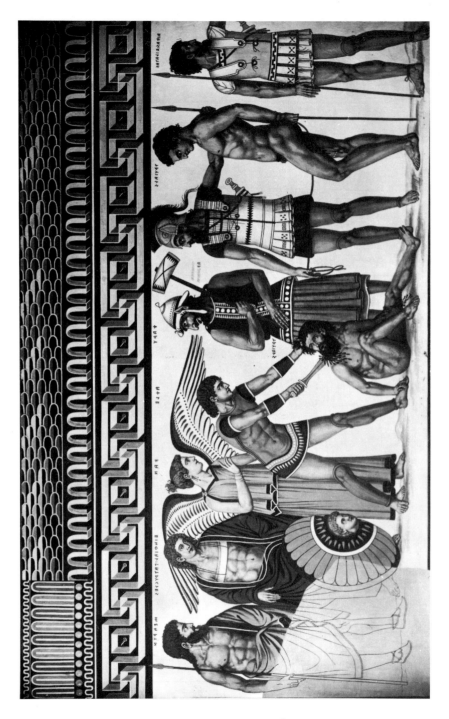

44. Painted inscription on tablets held by a winged figure on the wall of the Tomb of the Shields in Tarquinia. Fourth century B.C. (*TLE* 91; Cristofani 159–60, Staccioli No. 11).

> *zilci vel(u)s hulchniesi larth velchas*
> *vel(thur)s aprth(nal)c c(la)n sacnisa thui*
> *(ei)th suthith acazr*

'While 'praetor' was Vel Hulchnie, Larth Velcha of Velthur and of Aprthnai the son consecrated here in this tomb offerings (?)'
('During the 'praetorship' of Vel Hulchnie, Larth Velcha, son of Velthur and of Aprthnai, made offerings here in this tomb.').

45. Inscription on the wall of a tomb in Tarquinia (now lost). Second century B.C. (*TLE* 105; Cristofani 152; Staccioli 100):

> *vel aties velthurus lemnisa celati cesu*

'Vel Aties (the son) of Velthur (and) of Lemni in this cella lies'.
('Vel Aties, son of Velthur and of Lemni, lies in this cella'.)

46. Inscription painted on the wall of the Tomb of the Cardinal in Tarquinia. Second century B.C. (*TLE* 130, cf. 103; Staccioli No. 16):

> *ravnthus felcial felces arnthal larthial vipenal sethres cuthnas puia*

'Of Ravnthu Felci, of Felce Arnth (and) of Larthi Vipinai, of Sethre Cuthna the wife'.
('[This is the grave] of Ravnthu Felci, daughter of Arnth Felce and of Larthi Vipinai, wife of Sethre Cuthna'.)

47. Pillar from the Tomb of the Claudii in Cerveteri. Late fourth century B.C. (*CIE* 6213; Pallottino, *SE* 37 [1969] 69):

> *laris avle larisal clenar sval cn suthi cerichunce apac atic sanisva thui cesu clautiethurasi*

'Laris (and) Aulus, sons of Laris, (while) living made this tomb. Both father and mother, deceased (?), lie here. For the family (?) of the Claudii'.

(*suthi and sanisva* are written with the four-bar sigma, $\gtrsim$, typical of Cerveteri).

48. On the wall of a tomb at Tarquinia. Second century B.C. (*TLE* 888; Staccioli No. 14; Cristofani 155–6):

> *metli arnthi puia amce spitus larthal svalce avil LXIIII ci clenar acnanas arce*

'Metli Arnthi wife was of Spitu (the son) of Larth: (she) lived years sixty-four; three sons she had (arce?)'
('Metli Arnthi was the wife of Larth's son Spitu; she lived for sixty-four years; she had three sons'.)

49. Bronze model of a sheep's liver from the vicinity of Piacenza, inscribed with the names of Etruscan gods. Piacenza, Museo Civico. Hellenistic period. (*TLE* 719; van der Meer, *BABesch* 54 (1979) 49–64; Pfiffig, *Religio Etrusca* 121–7).

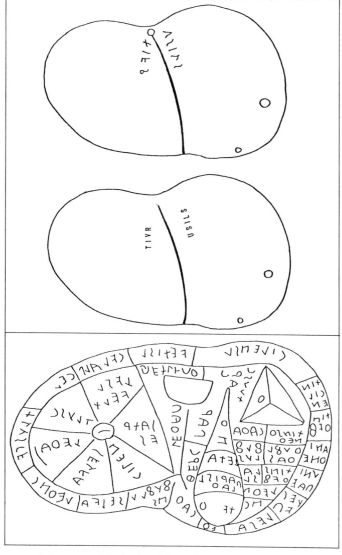

36 Bronze model of a sheep's liver from Piacenza (source 49)

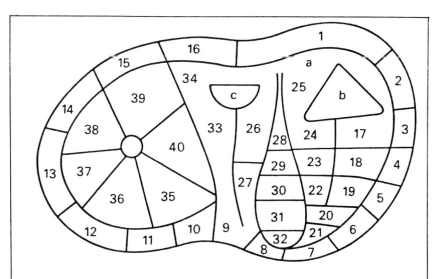

THE PIACENZA LIVER

a, gall bladder
b, caudate process
c, papillary process

Border

1 Cilensl	9 Caθ
2 Tin Cilen	10 Fufluns
3 Tin Θvf	11 Selva
4 Ani Θne	12 Leθns
5 Uni Mae	13 Tluscv
6 Tecvm	14 Cel
7 Leθn	15 Cvlalp
8 Eθ	16 Vetisl

Right Lobe

In the grid pattern:

17 Tinsθ Neθ	21 Nc
18 Θuflθas	22 Lasl
19 Tins Θvf	23 Fuflns
20 Leθn	24 Caθa

Around the gall bladder:

25 Mar Tlusc 27 Herc
26 Mari

On the gall bladder:

28 Θ	31 Marisl Laθ
29 N	32 Tv Θ
30 Leta	

Left Lobe

Outside the wheel pattern:

33 Letham 34 Θetlumθ

In the wheel pattern:

35 Cilcen	38 Tlusc
36 Selva	39 Lvsl Vel
37 Leθms	40 Satres

cath. eth. lethn. tecvm. uni mae. ani. thne. tin thvf.
tin cilen. cilensl. vetisl. cvl alp. cel. tluscv. lethns.
selva. fufluns. tinsth neth. catha. thuflthas. fuflns.
tins thvf. lasl. lethn. nc. tv( )th. marisl lath. leta.
np. th. tlusc mar. mari. herc. metlvmth. letham. satres.
lvsl velch. tlusc. lethms. selvan. cilen. usils. tivr.

There are twenty-one names of divinities, some of which can be identified: *tin* = Jupiter; *uni* = Juno; *catha* = sun god; *cel* = a mother goddess; *selvan* = Silvanus; *fufluns* = Bacchus; *herc* (*Hercle*) = Hercules; *usil* = the sun; *tivr* = the moon. Some are repeated (e.g. *tins, fufluns*) three, four or even five times. They are all native Etruscan gods. Greek gods represented on mirrors belong to mythology, art, and literature, not to ritual (fig. 36).

50. Funerary urn from Monteriggioni, near Siena. Second century B.C. (*TLE* 428; Cristofani 145; Staccioli 100, No. 17):

mi capra calisnaś larthal śepuś arnthalisla cursnialch
'I (am) the urn of Calisna (the son) of Larth Sepu, (grandson) of Arnth and of Cursni'.

51. Painted on the wall of a tomb at Tarquinia. Second century B.C. (*TLE* 890; Pfiffig, 226):

felsnas: la: lethes: svalce: avil: CVI: murce: capue: tleche: hanipaluscle:
'Felsnas, son of Larth Lethe, lived 106 years. (He) lived (?) at Capua. (He) was enrolled in (the army) of Hannibal'.

La is an abbreviation for Larth; *cf.* Latin *L* for *Lucius*, *C* for *Claudius*.)

52. Cast bronze coin, *aes grave* with Janus head. Beginning of third century B.C. (*TLE* 800; cf. *TLE* 367, *vatl.*):

velathri. 'Volterra'.

53. Inscription engraved on the life-size bronze statue called the 'Arringatore', 'the public speaker', offered as a public monument by his community. The statue was found in Umbrian territory, perhaps at Perugia, and dates to about 100 B.C. (*TLE* 651; Dohrn, *BdA* 1964, 97ff.; Cristofani 171–3).

auleśi . meteliś . ve(lus) . vesial . clenśi
cen . flereś . tece . sanśl . tenine . tuthineś . chisvlicś
'To Aulus Metellius, the son of Vel and Vesi, this statue set up, as a votive offering, Tenine (?) by deliberation (?) of the people'
('For Aulus Metellius, the son of Vel and Vesi, Tenine set up this statute as a votive offering, by deliberation of the people').

37 (a) Bronze statue of the Arringatore (b) Drawing of inscription on hem of toga (source 53)

(A connection of *tuthines* with the Umbrian word *tota* seems likely. *Tota* means 'the city', 'the community', 'the people'. Aulus Metellius had evidently deserved to have this statue set up as a civic honour. In this and in the following inscription note the genitive ending in ś, typical of northern Etruria) (fig. 37).

54. Sections of Etruscan text on the linen 'book' torn to make bandages for the mummy of a woman, now in Zagreb, National Museum. 150–100 B.C. (*TLE* 1; Pfiffig 244–50; Roncalli, *JdI* 95, 1980, 227–57). (fig. 38)

celi ('In the month of Cel') *huthiś zathrumiś* ('on the twenty-sixth [day]' *flerchva* ('the offerings') *nethunsl* ('to Neptune') *śucri* ('must be made (?)') *thezeri-c* ('and immolated') (VIII, 3)

> *cntnam thesan fler veiveś thezeri etnam aisna* [. . .] *ich huthiś zathrumiś*
> 'And the same morning the offering to Veiovis must be immolated and furthermore [. . .] the divine service as on the twenty-sixth (day)' (XI, 14)

'In the month of Celi (September), on the twenty-sixth day the offerings to Neptune must be made and immolated. And the same morning the offering to Veiovis must be immolated, and furthermore the divine service, as on the twenty-sixth day.'

> *tinśi, tiurim, avils*, 'day, month, year' (VIII, 15)

55. Three border markers with identical texts found in Tunisia between 1907 and 1915, set up by Etruscan colonists, perhaps from Chiusi, to designate the territory of a clan, tribe or village with the name *Dardanii*. Etruscan *termini* or boundaries were under the protection of Jupiter. The number 1000 indicates the size of the territory. The word *Dardanii*, 'Trojans', indicates Latin influence. Second or first century B.C. (perhaps 82 B.C.) (J. Heurgon, *CRAI* 1969, 526–51; H. S. Versnel, *Bibl. Orientalis* 33 (1976) 107). Written in Latin characters:

> M. UNATA. ZUTAŚ. TUL. DARDANIUM. TINŚ Φ

In Latin this would read:

> *Marce Unata Zutas. Fines Dardanium. Iouis. 1000 passuum*
> 'Marcus Unata Zutas. Boundaries of the Trojans. To Jupiter. 1000 paces'.

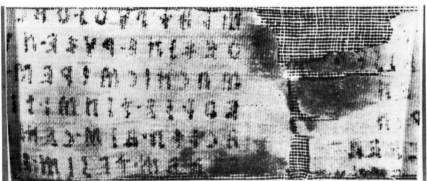

38 Zagreb mummy wrappings (source 54)

COMPARATIVE WORD CHART

Indoeuropean words

Meaning	Etruscan	Latin	Greek	Sanskrit
1. *Family Relationships*				
father	apa	pater	pātér	pitā́
mother	ati	māter	mātēr, métēr	mātā́
son	clan	fīlius	hyiós	sunúḥ
daughter	sech	fīlia	thygátēr	duhitā́
wife*	puia	mulier,	gynḗ	gnā́
		fēmina, uxor		
brother	ruva	frāter	(phrátēr)	bhrā́tā

*'Husband' does not appear in Etruscan texts because of the patriarchal way of life of the Etruscans.

2. *Religion and Law*				
Zeus, Jupiter	Tinia	Diēs (piter)	Zeús patḗr	Dyaúṣ pitā́
		Iouis,		
		Iu(ppiter)		
king	(lucumō)	rēx, rēgis	—	rā́jā
	lauchum			
god	ais, eis	deus	theós	deváḥ
(cf. 'divine')	aisar (pl.)	(deiuos:		
		archaic)		

Indoeuropean words

Meaning	Etruscan	Latin	Greek	Sanskrit
3. *Numerals*				
1 one	thu	oinos, ūnus	oínē	é(kaḥ)
2 two	zal	duo	dýo	dvá
3 three	ci	trēs	treîs	tráyaḥ
4 four	śa	quattuor	téttares	čatváraḥ
5 five	mach	quīnque	pénte	páñča
6 six	huth	sex	héx	ṣáṭ (sáṣ)
10 ten	śar	decem	déka	dáśa
20 twenty	zathrum	uīgintī	weíkosi	vimśatíḥ
30 thirty	cialch	trīgintā	triákonta	trimsát
50 fifty	muvalch	quinquāgintā	pentékonta	pancāśát

Note: It is clear from the comparative word chart that Etruscan consistently differs in basic vocabulary from the other languages here chosen to exemplify the Indoeuropean family of languages; Etruscan is not a member of the family – probably the only language of ancient Italy in historical times that was *not* a member.

GLOSSARY

*Words preceded by an asterisk are reconstructed from forms given by Greek and Roman authors. For further information see vocabulary lists in Pallottino, *Etruscans*; Pfiffig, *Etruskische Sprache*; and *Thesaurus Linguae Etruscae* I. *Indice Lessicale*.

A

ac⁄ = make, offer
acazr = objects offered in the tomb
acale (Aclus) = June
Achile, Achle = Achilles
Achmemrun = Agamemnon
Achrum = Acheron
ais, eis = god (aisar, eisar = gods)
aisna, eisna = divine, of the gods
Aita, Eita = Hades (Gk. Haides)
Aivas, Evas = Ajax
al⁄ = give, offer
Alchumena, Alcumena = Alcmene
Alichsantre, Alcsentre = (Paris)
   Alexander
alpan, alpnu = gift, offering; willingly
alphaze = offering
am⁄ = to be
Aminth = Cupid, Eros
an (ana, ane, anc, ananc) = he, she
Ane, Ani = Janus
apa = father
Apulu, Aplu = Apollo
ar⁄, er⁄ = to make, move
*arac = falcon

*arim = monkey
Aritimi, Artume = Artemis
ars⁄ = push away?
aska = name of vase (Gk. *askós*)
athre = building (Lat. *atrium*?)
ati, ativu = mother
ati nacna = grandmother
Atunis = Adonis
avil = year
Avile, Avle, Aule = Aulus

C

⁄c = and
ca = this
Cae, Cai = Caius, Gaius
camthi = name of magistracy
cape, capi = vase, container
   (cf. Lat. *capiō*?)
*capr⁄ = April
capra = urn
*capu = falcon
car⁄, cer⁄ = make, build
Caśntra = Cassandra
Castur = Castor
Catha = Sun, sun god
Catmite = Ganymede

cecha = ceremony (right, law): zilch
   cechaneri = title
cechase = name of magistracy
cehen = this one here
cela = room (Lat. *cella*)
celi = September
celu = priestly title
cep⟋, cepen = priestly title
ces⟋ = lie
cezp = 8?
cezpalch = 80?
cver, cvil = gift, offering
ci = 3
cialch⟋, cealch⟋ = 30
ciz = three times
clan, clenar (pl.) = son
cletram = basin, basket, cart for
   offerings (Umbrian *kletra*)
Clevsin⟋ = Chiusi
cleva = offering
Cluthumustha = Clytemnestra
Cneve = Cnaeus
culichna = vase, 'little kylix'
   (Gk. *kylix*)
cupe = cup (Gk. *kúpē*, Lat. *cupa*)

E

Easun, Eiasun = Jason
eca = see *ca*
Ectur, Echtur = Hector
eleivana = of oil: aska eleivana
   (Gk. *élaion*)
Elina, Elinai = Helen
⟋em = minus
enac, enach = then, afterwards
epl, pi, pul = in, to, up to
eslz = twice
etera, eteri = foreigner; slave, client
   (serf?)
etnam = and, also

V

vacal, vacil, vacl = libation?
Vanth = name of underworld goddess

Vecu, Vecui, Vecunia = name of a
   nymph
Vel = proper name (masc.)
*velcitna (Velcitanus) = March
vers⟋ = fire (or ladle?)
vinum, vinm = wine (lat. *uīnum*)

Z

zal, zel⟋, esal⟋ = 2
zathrum = 20
zeri = rite, legal action?
zich⟋ = to write
zil⟋ = to rule?
zil, zilc, zilach, zilath = a magistrate
   (Lat. *praetor*)
Ziumite = Diomedes
ziva = the dead, deceased

H

hec⟋, hech⟋ = put, place, add
Hercle = Herakles, Hercules
herme, hermu, herma, heramaśva =
   statue? (Gk. Hermes)
*hermi⟋ (gloss, Ermius) = August
hinthial = soul, ghost
hus⟋, husiur (pl.) = youth; children
huth = 6

Th (θ)

tham⟋ = to build, found
Thanachvil = Tanaquil (Thana +
   cvil, 'gift of Thana')
thapna = vase (for offerings?)
thaurch = funerary
thaure, thaura = tomb
Thefarie = Tiberius
Thesan = morning, dawn, Aurora
These = Theseus
Thevru Mineś = Minotaur (de
   Simone II, 95)
thez⟋ = to make an offering
thi = pronoun
thina = vase, *ōlla* (Lat. *tina*.
   Gk. *dínos*)

thu = one
thucte = name of month
thui = here, now
thunz = once

I

ic, ich, ichnac = as
ica = this
Ilithiia = Eileithyia
ilu⁄ = verb of offering or prayer
in, inc = it
ipa = relative pronoun
ipe ipa = whoever, whatever
ister = actor (gloss: Lat. *histrio*)
ita = this
*itu⁄ (gloss, *itus* or *ituare*) = to divide?

L

Larce, Laris, Larth = Lars
Larthi = proper name (fem.)
Lasa = nymph
lauchum = king (Lat. *lucumō*)
lauchumna = 'belonging to a lucumo',
    palace
lautni = 'of the family', freedman
lautnitha, lautnita = freedwoman
lautun, lautn = family, *gēns*
lechtum = name of vase (Gk. *lēkythos*)
lechtumuza = little lekythos
lein⁄ = to die?
leu = lion
lucair = to rule
lup⁄, lupu = to die

M

⁄m, ⁄um = and
mach = 5
Macstrna = Mastarna; Servius Tullius?
    (Lat. *magister?*)
macstrev = name of magistracy
mal⁄ = to give, dedicate?
malena, malstria = mirror
Mamarce, Mamerce = Mamercus
    (from Māmers, Oscan name of

Mars; cf. Oscan Mamercus)
man, mani = the dead (Lat. *Manes*)
manin⁄ = to offer to the Manes?
Marce = Marcus
maru, marunu = name of magistracy
    (Lat. *marō*, Umbr. *maron⁄*)
masan, masn = name of month?
matam, matan = above, before
math = honey, honeyed wine
mech = people, league
Menle = Menelaus
Menrva = Minerva
methlum = district
mi, mini = I, me
mul⁄ = to offer, dedicate as an ex⁄voto
mulach, malak, mlach = votive
    offering, dedication
mun⁄, muni = underground place,
    tomb
mur⁄ = stay, reside
murs = urn, sarcophagus
mutana, mutna = sarcophagus

N

nac = how, as, because
nefts, nefs, nefis = nephew, grandson
    (Lat. *nepos*)
nene = nurse, wet⁄nurse
neri = water
nesna = belonging to the dead?
nethsrac = haruspicina
netsvis = haruspex
nuna = offering?
nurph⁄ = 9?

P

Pacha = Bacchus, Dionysos
pachathur = Bacchante, maenad
pachie⁄, pachana = Bacchic
pacusnasie, pacusnasie = Bacchic,
    Dionysiac
papa = grandfather
papals = of the grandfather: grandson
patna = name of vase (Gk. *patane*,

Lat. *patina*?)
Patrucle = Patroclus
Pecse ⁻ Pegasus
penthuna, penthna = cippus, stone?
Perse = Perseus
pi = at, in, through
pruch, pruchum = jug (Gk. *próchous*)
prumathś, prumts = great-grandson
puia = wife
pul = see pi
Pultuce = Pollux
pulumchva = stars?
purth, purthne = name of magistrate
   or magistracy; dictator?
put-, puth- = vase, well? (Lat. *puteus*,
   puteal?)

Q

qutun, qutum = name of vase
   (Gk. *kōthōn*)

R

rach- = prepare
Ramutha, Ramtha = proper name
   (fem.)
Rasna = Etruscan, of Etruria
ratum = according to law
Ravnthu = proper name (fem.)
ril = at the age of . . . (years)
rumach = Roman
ruva = brother

S, Ś

śa = 4
sac- = carrying out a sacred act
sacni = sanctuary
sacnisa = consecrate?
sal- = make, carry out
śar = 10
sath-, śat- = put, establish, be put?
Satre = Saturn
śealch = 40
sec, sech = daughter
Selvan(s) = Silvanus

semph = 7?
semphalch = 70?
Sethlans = Vulcan
Sethre = proper name (masc.)
snenath = maid, companion (fem.)
sval = alive; to live
spur- = city
spurana, spureni = having to do with
   the city
Spurie = Spurius
śran, sren = ornament, figure
srencve = decorated with figures?
suplu = flutist (Lat. *sūbulō*)
śuth-, sut- = to stay, place?
śuthi = seat, tomb
śuthina = sepulchral gift

T

ta = this
tamera = name of magistracy
Tarchi = proper name (masc.)
Tarchun = Tarchon
ten- = to act as
tes-, tesam- = to care for
tesinth = caretaker
teta = grandmother
tev- = to show, see?
tevarath = on-looker, judge at the
   games, umpire
tin- = day
Tin, Tinia = Jupiter, Zeus, god of
   daylight
Tite = Titus
tiu, tiv-, tiur = moon, month
Tlamu = Telamon
tmia = place, sacred building
-tnam = see etnam
trin- = to plead, supplicate
Truia = Troy?
Truials = Trojan
truth, trut = libation
trutnuth, trutnvt = priest (*fulguriator*)
Tuchulcha = name of a demon
tul = stone

tular, tularu = boundaries
tunur = one at a time
tur⁄ = to give
tura = incense
Turan = Venus, Aphrodite
Turmś = Mercury
turza = offering
tuś = funerary niche
tusurthir = married couple? ('in the double urn'?)
tuthi, tuti⁄ = community, state (Umbr. *tota*?)
tuthin, tuthina⁄ = of the state, public

U

Uni = Juno, Hera
Urphe = Orpheus
Urusthe = Orestes
Usil = Sun (Lat. *Aurēlius*?)
uslane = at noon
ut⁄ = carry out, perform
Utusthe, Uthste = Odysseus, Ulysses

P

Pherse = Perseus

Phersipnai = Persephone, Proserpina
Phersu = mask, masked person, actor (Lat. *persona*)

Ch (χ)

Chalchas = Calchas
Charu, Charun = name of demon
Chosfer = October (gloss)

F

*falatu (gloss, *falado*) = sky
fan⁄ = to consecrate?
fanu = sacred place (Lat. *fānum*?)
favi = grave, temple vault (Lat. *fauissa*?)
fler = offering, sacrifice
flerchva = ceremony, sacrifice
flere = divinity, god
flereś = statue
frontac = interpreter of lightning; see trutnuth (Gk. *Brontē*?)
Fufluna = Populonia
Fufluns = Dionysos, Bacchus, Liber (Lat. *populus*?)

MYTHOLOGICAL FIGURES

The following is intended as a concise listing of Etruscan mythological figures which do not have close counterparts in Greek mythology. Many of these are known from scenes engraved on bronze mirrors. In *A Guide to Etruscan Mirrors*, ed. N. T. de Grummond (Tallahassee 1982) Ch. VII, Cheryl Sowder lists these figures in English alphabetical order with a full description for each. The reader will also find references to figures appearing on mirrors and elsewhere in Pfiffig, *Religio Etrusca*, and de Simone, *Entlehnungen*. The Etruscan counterparts of Greek divinities and heroes, such as Tinia, Menrva, Uni, etc., have been included in the Glossary above.

Achvizr (Achuvesr, Achuvizr, Achviztr)　A figure sometimes male, sometimes female, associated with the circle of Turan; also represented in the company of Achilles, Thetis, and Alpan. (*ES* 4.322; 4.25).

Alpan (Alpanu, Alpnu)　Represented on several mirrors; may stand for the Greek Harmonia or the Roman Concordia. The word seems to mean 'willingly' (*ES* 4.322).

Althaia　May correspond to the Greek Aithra, Helen's serving maid; shown on a mirror with the Judgment of Paris (*Guide to Etruscan Mirrors*, pl. 50–1).

Cacu　Singer or seer appearing on a mirror with the boy Artile as his attendant; the two are about to be ambushed by two soldiers, Caile and Avle Vipinas. The story is obscure, but may be connected to an episode involving Cacus and Marsyas (*ES* 5.127).

Calaina　The Etruscan name of a Nereid appearing as a companion of Thetis, perhaps corresponding to the Greek Galane (*ES* 5.96).

Celsclan　'Son of Cel (goddess of the sun)'; he appears on a mirror, pursued by the armed Laran (*ES* 5.84).

Chalchas   The name is that of the Greek seer Calchas. The Etruscan figure is winged and shown reading entrails. (*ES* 2.23).

Charun   Though the name translates the Greek Charon, the boatman of the Underworld, the Etruscan figure fulfils a different function; together with Vanth, he guides the dead to the Underworld. His attribute is the hammer (Pallottino, *Etruscan Painting*, pl. p. 117).

Chelphun   Name of a Silenus. Perhaps related to Greek *chalepós*, 'harsh', 'mischievous', 'dangerous' (*ES* 4.314).

Culsu   Along with Tuchulcha and Charun, this female demon appears on sarcophagi, funerary urns, and tomb paintings, but not on mirrors. (Brunn-Körte, *I rilievi della urne etrusche*, 3.98, 12).

Epiur (Epeur)   A child or youth whom Hercle protects and presents to Tinia or Menrva (*ES* 2.181).

Ethausva   A female divinity, perhaps the one referred to as *eth* on the liver from Piacenza, Ethausva appears on a mirror representing the birth of Menrva from the head of Tinia (*ES* 5.6).

Eurphia   A nymph or a Muse shown dancing in front of the youth Phaun (*ES* 5.32).

Euturpa (Euterpe)   Euturpa is the Etruscan spelling of the Greek Euterpē, the name of one of the Muses. On several mirrors she appears to represent a personification of love or pleasure, something like one of the Greek Charites (*ES* 2.188).

Evan   Appears once as a young woman, another time as a young man, in the circle of Turan and Atunis (*ES* 5.28).

Laran   A male figure on a number of mirrors, usually as a spectator, often armed. Once he pursues Celsclan (*ES* 5.84).

Lasa   Probably a generic term, something like a nymph; often associated with the circle of Turan. The name is often used with an epithet, e.g., *lasa sitmica, lasa racuneta* (*ES* 2.181; 5.24).

Leinth   Appears on two mirrors, once as a young woman, once as a youth. The name may be related to the verb *lein*, 'die' (*ES* 2.141; 2.166).

Malavisch   Appears on a number of mirrors, where she is being dressed by her attendants. She may be a bride being prepared for her wedding (an appropriate scene for a mirror) (*ES* 2.211–3).

Mariś   As in the case of Lasa, this name is used in conjunction with other names, or epithets (*mariś musta, mariś turan, mariś halna, mariś husrnana, mariś isminthians*). His character is not easy to define; he appears as a bearded man, as a youth, and even as a group of babies tended by Menrva. The name appears twice on the Piacenza liver, once on the lead tablet from

Magliano (*ES* 3.257b; 5.1).

Mean (Meanpe) A female figure who appears on a number of mirrors, usually in a secondary supporting role; perhaps the Etruscan equivalent of Nike or Victoria, since she crowns someone with a wreath (*ES* 2.141).

Mlacuch A young woman abducted by Herakles on a mirror; the story is otherwise unknown and thus constitutes a purely Etruscan version of one of the exploits of Herakles (*ES* 4.344).

Munthuch (Munthch, Munthu) The name is probably related to *munth*, equivalent to Latin *mundus*, Greek *kosmos*, 'adornment' or 'order'. She appears as an attendant in adornment scenes on mirrors (*ES* 2.213).

Nathum Probably an Etruscan version of a Fury, shown holding snakes, watching Urusthe (Orestes) killing his mother, Cluthumustha (Clytemnestra) (*ES* 2.238).

Phaun (Faun) Shown as an Apollo-like youth playing the lyre. The name is that of the Greek Phaon, the boatman to whom Aphrodite gave eternal youth and beauty (*ES* 5.32).

Phulsphna Young woman appearing as a spectator as Helen flees from Menelaus armed with a sword (*ES* 4.398).

Preale Male figure, a spectator in a scene of the birth of Menrva (*ES* 4.284.1).

Pulthisph Youth present at the embrace of Turan and Atunis (*ES* 1.111).

Rescial (Recial, Reschualc). A young woman, something like a Lasa, who appears on several mirrors. The name may be related to *sval*, 'live' (compare *lein*, perhaps related to *leinth*) (*ES* 5.96).

Sime The name of a satyr, clearly a translation of the Greek *Símos*, 'snub-nosed' (*ES* 4.299).

Snenath A young woman in the circle of Turan. One mirror shows *snenath tur(a)ns*, suggesting that perhaps *snenath* is a word meaning 'maid servant' or 'companion' (compare *acila* = *ancilla*, 'handmaiden', on a Praenestine mirror) (*ES* 1.111; 5.151).

Tages According to Etruscan mythology known through Greek and Latin sources, Tages was a prophetic child who sprang up from a freshly ploughed furrow at Tarquinia and gave out rules of divination and religion, which were then recorded and became the basis of the *etrusca disciplina* (Herbig, *Götter und Dämonen der Etrusker*, 30).

Tarchunus (Tarchon) The legendary founder of Tarquinii, he appears on a mirror dressed as a *haruspex*, watching Pava Tarchies examining a liver for omens. According to one version of the Tages legend, Tarchon was the one who recorded Tages' prophetic song (Brendel, *Etruscan Art*, fig. 316).

Thalna (Thalana)   A popular figure on Etruscan mirrors, she appears at scenes of love-making and child-birth (*ES* 1.66).

Thanr   This divinity, shown on mirrors representing divine births and babies (Menrva, Epiur), seems to have been worshipped in Etruria (*ES* 5.6).

Tiphanati   A minor figure, shown with Atunis on one mirror (*ES* 1.116).

Tuchulcha   Like Charun, a bestial, terrifying demon of death, with vulture's beak, donkey's ears and writhing snakes. In the Underworld in the Tomb of Orcus at Tarquinia he appears next to Theseus (Herbig, *Götter und Dämonen der Etrusker*, pl. 41.1).

Tusna   The swan of Turan (*ES* 4.322).

Vanth   A female demon of the Underworld, Vanth often appears together with Charun on sarcophagi, urns, and wall paintings, more rarely on mirrors. She is present at, but not involved in death, and sometimes is given the role of a Greek Fury (*ES* 5.110).

Vipinas, Avle and *Caile*   These two brothers, known from Latin sources as Aulus and Caelius Vibenna, and connected with Mastarna (Servius Tullius), seem to have been real historical characters who were regarded as national heroes in Etruscan legend. They were represented in the François Tomb at Vulci, and with Cacu on an engraved mirror, and their names appear in a dedication (Sources 35, 43, figs. 29, 35).

Zipna (Zipanu, Zip(n)a, Sipna)   Female figure on several mirrors, connected with the circle of Turan (*ES* 4.322).

NAMES OF CITIES

MODERN	ETRUSCAN	LATIN
Arezzo	Arēt⁄(?)	Arrētium
Bologna	Felsina	Bonōnia
Bolsena (Orvieto?)	Velsu, Velsna, Velzna⁄	Volsiniī
Capua	Capua, Capeva	Capua
Cerveteri (*Caere Vetus,*	Chaire, Cheri,	Caere (then *Caere Vetus*)
'ancient Caere')	Chaisrie, Cisra	(Greek *Agylla*)
Cesena	Ceisna	Caesēna
Chiusi	Clevsin, Clevsina	Clusium, Camars
Cortona	Curtun	Cortōna
Fiesole	Vi(p)sul	Faesulae
Ischia	Inarimē	Pitecusa (Greek
		Pithekoussaî)
Magliano	Hepa(?)	Heba
Mantova, Mantua	Manthva	Mantua
Modena	Mutina	Mutina
Perugia	Per(u)sna	Perusia
(Poggio Buco)	Statna	Statōnia
Populonia	Pupluna, Fufluna	Populōnia
Ravenna	Rav(e)na(?)	Rauenna
Rimini	Arimna	Ariminum
Roma	Ruma	Rōma
Siena	Saena(?), Sena	Saena
Sovana	Sveama⁄, Suana	Suana
Sutri	Suthri	Sutrium
Tarquinia	Tarch(u)na	Tarquiniī
Talamone	Tlamu	Telamōn

MODERN	ETRUSCAN	LATIN
Tuscania	Tusc(a)na	Tuscāna
Veio, Veii	Veia	Veiī
Vetulonia	Vatluna, Vetluna	Vetulōnia
Viterbo?	Sur(i)na	Surrīna
Volterra	Velathri	Volaterrae
Vulci	Velch, Velc(a)l	Vulcī

Sources: Pfiffig, *Einführung* 92–3; Pallottino, 'Nomi etruschi di città', *Saggi di Antichità*, 710–26.

NAMES OF THE MONTHS

January	?
February	?
March	*Velcitanus* or *Velistanus*
April	*Cabreas* (**capre*)
May	*Ampiles* or *Amphiles*
June	*Aclus* (*acale*)
July	?
August	*Ermius*
September	*Caelius* or *Celius* (*celi*)
October	*Chosfer*
November	?
December	?

Note: The names of the months listed above are mostly known to us from glosses; no doubt they were used in ritual calendars. Forms ending in ⸗*us* (e.g. *Velcitanus, Aclus*) have been Latinized. The month of *Masn*, or *Masan* (Pyrgi tablet, Zagreb mummy text, source 54), has not yet been identified, nor has *Thucte*.

Other words signifying dates include: *itus*, 'the Ides'; *tin*, 'day' (also the name of the god Tinia); *tiu, tiv* or *tiur⸗* 'moon' and also 'month' (also the name of the moon goddess). The text of the Zagreb mummy (source 54) reads (VI): *eslem zathrumiś acale tinśin*, where *tinśin* means 'in the day' (*tin*), *acale* the month, and *eslem zathrumiś* is a numeral (18): 'the eighteenth day of June'.

ABBREVIATIONS

AGI   *Archivio Glottologico Italiano*

AJA   *American Journal of Archaeology*

AJAH   *American Journal of Ancient History*

ANRW   *Aufstieg und Niedergang der Römischen Welt.* Berlin, New York, 1972–

ArchClass   *Archeologia Classica*

Aufnahme 1981   *Aufnahme fremder Kultureinflüsse in Etrurien und das Problem des Retardierens in der etruskischen Kunst. Schriften des Deutschen Archäologen-Verbandes* 5. Mannheim 1981. With contributions on language by H. Rix, C. de Simone

Banti   L. Banti, *The Etruscan Cities and Their Culture.* Berkeley, Los Angeles, 1973

Brendel   O. J. Brendel, *Etruscan Art.* Harmondsworth, 1978

BSL   *Bulletin de la Société de Linguistique de Paris*

BABesch   *Bulletin van de Vereeniging tot Bevordering der Kennis van de Antieke Beschaving*

Canciani–von Hase, *Tomba Bernardini*   F. Canciani, F.-W. von Hase, *La tomba Bernardini di Palestrina.* (*Latium Vetus* II). Rome 1979

Caratteri dell'Ellenismo   *Caratteri dell'Ellenismo nelle urne etrusche. Prospettiva,* Suppl. I. Florence 1977

CIE   *Corpus Inscriptionum Etruscarum*

Civiltà del Lazio Primitivo   *Civiltà del Lazio Primitivo.* Rome 1976

Colonna, 'Sistema alfabetico'   G. Colonna, 'Il sistema alfabetico', in *L'etrusco arcaico,* Florence, 1976, 7–24

CP   *Classical Philology*

CRAI   *Comptes Rendus de l'Académie des Inscriptions et Belles Lettres*

Cristofani   M. Cristofani, *L'Arte degli Etruschi. Produzione e consumo.* Turin 1978

Cristofani, *Etruscans* M. Cristofani, *The Etruscans*. London 1979
Cristofani, *Introduzione* M. Cristofani, *Introduzione allo studio dell'etrusco*.
Florence 1978
DdA *Dialoghi di Archeologia*
Dumézil, *ARR* G. Dumézil, *Archaic Roman Religion*. Chicago 1970
ES E. Gerhard, *Etruskische Spiegel*. Berlin, 1840–97
Helbig, *Führer*[4] W. Helbig, *Führer durch die öffentlichen Sammlungen
klassischer Altertümer in Rom*, vols. 1–4, ed. H. Speier. Tübingen
1963–72
IBR D. Ridgway, F. R. S. Ridgway, eds., *Italy Before the Romans*.
London, New York, San Francisco 1979
Iscriz. prelatine *Atti dei convegni Lincei*, 39. *Le iscrizioni prelatine in Italia*.
Roma, 1977 [1979], edited by G. Bonfante
JdI *Jahrbuch des Deutschen Archäologischen Instituts*
JHS *Journal of Hellenic Studies*
JRS *Journal of Roman Studies*
Kaimio (K.) J. Kaimio, 'The Ousting of Etruscan by Latin in Etruria',
Studies in the Romanization of Etruria. *Acta Instituti Romani Finlandiae V*.
Rome, 1972, 85–245
Klein, *Etym. Dict.* E. Klein, *Comprehensive Etymological Dictionary of the
English Language*. Amsterdam 1971
Macnamara, *Everyday Life* E. Macnamara, *Everyday Life of the Etruscans*.
London and New York 1973
MEFRA *Mélanges d'Archéologie et d'Histoire de l'École Française de Rome*
Mélanges Heurgon *L'Italie préromaine et la Rome républicaine. Mélanges offerts à
J. Heurgon*. Rome 1976
Ogilvie R. M. Ogilvie, *Commentary on Livy I–V*. Oxford 1965
Out of Etruria L. Bonfante, *Out of Etruria. Etruscan Influence North and
South*. BAR International Series S103. Oxford 1981. With two
chapters on language by G. Bonfante
Pallottino M. Pallottino, *The Etruscans*. Harmondsworth 1978
Pfiffig A. J. Pfiffig, *Die etruskische Sprache*. Graz, 1969
Pfiffig, *Religio Etrusca (Rel.)* A. J. Pfiffig, *Religio Etrusca*. Graz, 1975
Pirgi *Scavi nel santuario etrusco di Pirgi*. Rome 1964
Popoli e Civiltà (Pop. e Civ.) *Popoli e civiltà dell'Italia antica* 1–7. Rome,
1974–8
PP *Parola del Passato*
REL *Revue des Études Latines*
REE Rivista di Epigrafia Etrusca, in *Studi Etruschi*

Ridgway, *CAH*   D. Ridgway, *The Etruscans*. Occasional Paper 6. Edinburgh, 1981. Chapter written for the *Cambridge Ancient History*

RömMitt (RM)   *Mitteilungen des Deutschen Archäologischen Instituts. Römische Abteilung*

Studi Pisani   *Studi linguistici in onore di V. Pisani*. Brescia 1969

StEtr (SE)   *Studi Etruschi*

Thesaurus   *Thesaurus Linguae Etruscae* I. Indice Lessicale. Rome 1978

TLE   M. Pallottino, *Testimonia Linguae Etruscae*. Second edition, Florence 1968

BIBLIOGRAPHY

I ARCHAEOLOGICAL INTRODUCTION

(See footnotes to this section for specialized works. The following are recommended for further reading.)

Aspetti e problemi dell'Etruria interna. Atti dell'VIII Congresso di Studi Etruschi e Italici, Orvieto 1972. Florence, 1974.

Banti, L. *The Etruscan Cities and their Culture.* Berkeley and Los Angeles, 1973.

Bianchi Bandinelli, R. and Giuliano, A. *Etruschi e Italici prima del dominio di Roma.* Milan, 1973.

Boitani, F., Cataldi, M., Pasquinucci, M., Torelli, M., and Coarelli, F. (ed.). *Etruscan Cities.* Milan, 1974.

Bonfante, L. *Etruscan Dress.* Baltimore and London, 1975. Abbr. *ED*
——[Warren], L. 'Roman triumphs and Etruscan kings: the changing face of the triumph', *JRS* 60 (1970) 49–66.

Brendel, O. J. *Etruscan Art.* Harmondsworth, 1978.

Cristofani, M. *L'Arte degli Etruschi. Produzione e consumo.* Turin, 1978.
——. *The Etruscans.* London, 1979.

Dennis, G. *The Cities and Cemeteries of Etruria.* 3rd edn. London, 1883.

Foresti, L. Aigner. *Tesi, ipotesi e considerazioni sull'origine degli Etruschi.* Vienna, 1974.

Grant, M. *The Etruscans.* New York, 1980.

Harris, W. V. *Rome in Etruria and Umbria.* Oxford, 1971.

Heurgon, J. *The Daily Life of the Etruscans.* New York, 1964.

Macnamara, E. *Everyday Life of the Etruscans.* London and New York, 1973.

Mansuelli, G. *The Art of Etruria and Early Rome.* New York, 1967.

Müller, K. O. and Deecke, W. *Die Etrusker.* Revised by A. J. Pfiffig.

Graz, 1965. Originally published in Stuttgart, 1877.

Ogilvie, R. M. *A Commentary on Livy, Books 1–5.* Oxford, 1965.

———. *Early Rome and the Etruscans.* Fontana History of the Ancient World. Atlantic Highlands, New Jersey, 1976.

Pallottino, M. *Etruscan Painting.* Geneva, 1951.

———. *The Etruscans.* Revised and enlarged edition, edited by D. Ridgway. Harmondsworth, 1978.

Potter, T. W. *The Changing Landscape of South Etruria.* London, 1979.

Prayon, F. *Frühetruskische Grab- und Hausarchitektur.* Heidelberg, 1975.

Richardson, E. H. *The Etruscans.* Chicago, 1964.

Ridgway, D. *The Etruscans.* Department of Archaeology, University of Edinburgh, Occasional Paper 6. Edinburgh, 1981. Chapter written for *The Cambridge Ancient History.*

——— and Ridgway, F. R. S., eds. *Italy Before the Romans.* London, New York and San Francisco, 1979.

Scullard, H. H. *The Etruscan Cities and Rome.* Ithaca, New York and London, 1967.

Sprenger, M. and Bartoloni, G. *Die Etrusker: Kunst und Geschichte.* Munich, 1977.

Torelli, M. *Etruria.* Guida Archeologica Laterza. Rome, 1980.

Vacano, O. W. von. *The Etruscans in the Ancient World.* Bloomington, Indiana, 1960.

II LANGUAGE – GRAMMAR, EPIGRAPHY

Books

Bonfante, L. *Out of Etruria. Etruscan Influence North and South,* BAR International Series 103 (1981), with two chapters on language by G. Bonfante.

Buonamici, G. *Epigrafia etrusca.* Florence, 1932.

Caffarello, N. *Avviamento allo studio della lingua etrusca.* Florence, 1975. Student handbook.

Corpus Inscriptionum Etruscarum (CIE), begun in 1893 by Pauli. The latest volume is M. Cristofani, *CIE,* II, 1, 4. Florence, 1970. For list of reviews, see M. Cristofani, *IBR* 408, n. 3. Also reviewed by L. Bonfante, *JRS* 66 (1976) 243–4. See also M. Cristofani, 'CIE II, 1, 4: Addenda e corrigenda', *StEtr* 44 (1976) 187–99.

Cristofani, M. *Introduzione allo studio dell'etrusco.* Florence, 1978. Useful handbook, with contemporary linguistic approach. Reviewed by G.

Bonfante, *AGI* 61 (1976) 268–77; A. J. Pfiffig, *Gnomon* 47 (1975) 418–420.

D'Aversa, A. *La lingua degli etruschi*. Brescia, 1979. Student handbook.

Devoto, G. *Le origini indoeuropee*. Florence, 1962.

L'etrusco arcaico. Atti del colloquio, Firenze, 1974. Florence, 1976. Specialized discussions, by G. Colonna, C. de Simone, M. Cristofani, M. Pallottino and others.

Fiesel, E. *Namen des griechischen Mythos im Etruskischen*. Göttingen, 1928. Pioneering study of Greek mythological names in Etruscan. Reviewed by E. Benveniste, *Revue de philologie, de littérature et d'histoire anciennes* 56 (1930) 67–75.

Die Göttin von Pyrgi, Akten des Kolloquiums zum Thema. Archäo-logische, linguistische und religionsgeschichtliche Aspekte, Tübingen, 1979. Florence, 1981. With contributions by M. Pallottino, G. Colonna, F. Prayon, M. Cristofani, C. de Simone, H. Rix, A. Tovar, R. Bloch, I. Krauskopf, O./W. von Vacano.

Guarducci, M. *Epigrafia Greca, I*. Rome, 1967.

Harris, W. V. *Rome in Etruria and Umbria*. Oxford, 1971.

Hermeneus 45 (1973–74). Special issue on the Etruscans.

Jeffery, L. H. *The Local Scripts of Archaic Greece*. Oxford, 1961.

Lambrechts, R. *Essai sur les magistratures des républiques étrusques*. Inst. Hist. Belge de Rome 7. Brussels, 1959.

Le lamine di Pirgi. Tavola rotonda internazionale, Roma 1968. Accademia Nazionale dei Lincei, Quaderno No. 147. Rome, 1970.

La Naissance de Rome. Paris, Petit Palais, 1977. Exhibition Catalogue.

Olzscha, K. *Interpretation der Agramer Mumienbinde*. Leipzig, 1939.

Pallottino, M. *Elementi di lingua etrusca*. Florence, 1936. (Basic: Etruscan phonetics, morphology and syntax.)

———. *The Etruscans*. Harmondsworth, 1978. (Part 3: The Etruscan Language, 187–234, is basic.)

———. *La langue étrusque: problèmes et perspectives*. Translated, and with an introduction by J. Heurgon, Paris, 1978.

——— *Testimonia Linguae Etruscae (TLE)*. 2nd edn. Florence, 1968. Indispensable collection of all important Etruscan texts, listed by provenance.

Pfiffig, A. J. *Einführung in die Etruskologie – Probleme, Methoden, Ergebnisse*. Darmstadt, 1972. Concise sketch of questions and controversies.

———. *Die etruskische Sprache*. Graz, 1969. Most recent and complete grammar, with full bibliography. Reviewed by C. Battisti, *Atene e Roma*

n.s. 16 (1971) 103–12; C. de Simone, *Kratylos* 14 (1969) 91–100; G.
Bonfante, *AGI* 56 (1971) 167–72; R. Pfister, *Gnomon* 44 (1972) 18–25;
H. Rix, *Göttingische Gelehrte Anzeigen* 277 (1975) 117–43.

Pieri, S. *Toponomastica della Toscana meridionale.* Siena, 1969. Revised by G.
Bonfante.

Pisani, V. *Le lingue dell'Italia antica oltre il latino.* 2nd edn. Turin, 1964.
(Useful study.)

Le ricerche epigrafiche e linguistiche sull'etrusco. Atti del colloquio, Firenze 1969.
Florence, 1973.

Ridgway, D. and Ridgway, F. R. S., eds. *Italy Before the Romans.* London,
New York and San Francisco, 1979. (See especially, Part Four,
'Aspects of the Etruscans', 239–412.)

Rix, H. *Das etruskische Cognomen.* Wiesbaden, 1963. (Model socio-
linguistic study of Etruscan names.)

Scavi nel santuario etrusco di Pirgi. Rome, 1964.

Simone, C. de. *Die griechischen Entlehnungen im Etruskischen,* I–II.
Wiesbaden, 1968–70. (Basic for archaeologists as well as linguists: list,
discussion and bibliography of mythological names on Etruscan mirrors
and other monuments.)

Slotty, F. *Beiträge zur Etruskologie.* Heidelberg, 1952.

Staccioli, R. A. *Il 'mistero' della lingua etrusca.* Rome, 1977. (Brief, popular
treatment, with useful illustrations and texts.)

Thesaurus Linguae Etruscae. I. Indice lessicale. Edited by M. Pallottino, with
M. Pandolfini Angeletti, C. de Simone, M. Cristofani and A.
Morandi. Rome, 1978. (Lexical index, beautifully edited. Lists
Etruscan words with provenance and publication.)

Torelli, M. *Elogia Tarquiniensia.* Florence, 1975. On epitaphs of members of
the Spurinna family and the Tomba dell'Orco in Tarquinia. Reviewed
by J. Heurgon, *StEtr* 46 (1978) 617–23; T. J. Cornell, *JRS* 68 (1978)
167–73. Abbr. *ET.*

Articles

Bizzarri, M., 'La necropoli di Crocifisso del Tufo a Orvieto', *StEtr* 30
(1962) 136–51.

Blakeway, A., 'Demaratus', *JRS* 25 (1935) 129–48.

Bloch, R., 'Étrusques et Romains', in *L'Écriture et la psychologie des peuples.*
Centre international, XXIIᵉ semaine de synthèse. Paris, 1963, 182ff.
[Work not seen by the authors.]

Bonfante, G., 'La pronuncia della *z* in etrusco', *StEtr* 36 (1968) 57–64; and 'Ancora la *z* etrusca', *StEtr* 37 (1969) 499–500.

——, 'Arezzo e gli Etruschi', in *Atti e Memorie dell'Accademia Petrarca di Lettere, Arti e Scienze di Arezzo* n.s. 41 (1973–5) [1977] 378–82.

——, 'Language and alphabet', in L. Bonfante, *Out of Etruria*. BAR International Series 103 (1981) 111–34.

——, 'The origin of the Latin name-system', *Mélanges Marouzeau* (Paris 1948) 43–59.

——, 'Problemi delle glosse etrusche' (riassunto), in *X Convegno di Studi Etruschi e Italici, Grosseto 1975. Atti*. Florence, 1977, 84.

——, review of A. J. Pfiffig, *Die etruskische Sprache* (1969), *AGI* 56 (1971) 167–72.

——, review of M. Cristofani, *Introduzione allo studio dell'etrusco* (1973), *AGI* 61 (1976) 268–77.

Bonfante, L., 'Appendix. Vocabulary', in *Etruscan Dress*. Baltimore, 1975, 101–4.

—— [Warren], L. 'Roman triumphs and Etruscan kings: the Latin word *Triumphus*', in *Out of Etruria*. BAR International Series 103 (1981) 93–110. Originally published 1970.

Brandenstein, W., 'Die Tyrrhenische stele von Lemnos', *Mitteilungen der Altorientalischen Gesellschaft* 7. Leipzig, 1934, 1–51.

——, *Real Encyclopädie* 7 (1948), 1920 ff. s.v. 'Tyrrhener'.

Camporeale, G., 'Sull'alfabeto di alcune iscrizioni etrusche arcaiche'. *Parola del Passato* 112 (1967) 227–35.

Colonna, G., 'Appendice I. I dadi "di Tuscania"', *StEtr* 46 (1978) 115. On the early history of the dice: they were *not* from Tuscania, but more probably from Vulci.

——, 'Firme arcaiche di artefici nell'Italia centrale', *RM* 82 (1975) 181–92.

——, 'La dea etrusca Cel e il santuario del Trasimeno', *Rivista di Storia Antica* 6–7 (1976–7) 45–62.

——, 'Nome gentilizio e società', *StEtr* 45 (1977) 175–92.

——, 'Nomi etruschi di vasi', *ArchClass* 25–6 (1973–4) 132–50.

——, 'Scriba cum rege sedens', in *Mélanges Heurgon*. Rome, 1976, 187–95.

——, 'Una nuova iscrizione etrusca del VII secolo e appunti sull'epigrafia ceretana dell'epoca', *MEFRA* 82 (1970) 637–72.

Cornell, T. J., '*Principes* of Tarquinia'. Review of *Elogia Tarquiniensia*, by M. Torelli. *JRS* (1978) 167–73.

Cortsen, S. P., 'L'inscription de Lemnos', *Latomus* 2 (1938) 3ff.

Cristofani, M., 'Appunti sull'epigrafia etrusca arcaica', *Annali della Scuola Normale di Pisa* 38 (1969) 99–113.

_____, 'Il "dono" nell'Etruria arcaica', *Parola del Passato* 30 (1975) 132–52.

_____, 'Note di epigrafia etrusca', *StEtr* 47 (1979) 157–61.

_____, Rapporto sulla diffusione della scrittura nell' Italia antica', *Scrittura e Civiltà* 2 (1978) 5–33.

_____, 'Recent advances in Etruscan epigraphy and language', in D. and F. R. S. Ridgway, eds., *Italy Before the Romans*. London, New York and San Francisco, 1979, 373–412. Basic: update on methods, trends, and results, with critical bibliography.

_____, 'Società e istituzioni nell'Italia preromana', *Popoli e civiltà dell'Italia antica* 7 (1978) 53–112, esp. 67–99. On Etruscan titles (*zilach, marunu,* etc.) and their significance; political, legal and social status of the *lautni,* 'libertus'. Important discussion and bibliography.

_____, 'Sull'origine e la diffusione dell'alfabeto etrusco', in *Aufstieg und Niedergang der römischen Welt* I, 2. Berlin and New York, 1972, 466–89. On the alphabet in Italy and Europe.

_____ and Phillips, K. M., 'Poggio Civitate: Etruscan letters and chronological observations', *StEtr* 39 (1971) 409–30.

Devine, A. M., 'Etruscan language studies and the aspirates', *StEtr* 42 (1974) 123–51.

Devoto, G., 'Il latino di Roma', *Popoli e civiltà dell'Italia antica* 6 (1978) 469–85, esp. 480–1, 'La comunità culturale etrusco-laziale', and 485, notes 57–62.

Dumézil, G., 'Appendix. Etruscan religion', in his *Archaic Roman Religion*. Chicago, 1970, 623–96.

Durante, M., 'Una sopravvivenza etrusca in latino', *StEtr* 41 (1973) 193–200.

Ernout, A., 'Les éléments étrusques du vocabulaire latin', *Bulletin de la Sociéte de linguistique* 30 (1930) 82ff.

Forni, G., 'Le tribù romane nelle bilingui etrusco-latine e greco-latine', *Studi Betti* (1961) 195–207, esp. 203.

Garbini, G., 'Lingua etrusca e aritmetica', *Parola del Passato* 20 (1975) 345–55.

Heurgon, J., 'La coupe d'Aulus Vibenna', in *Mélanges J. Carcopino*. Paris, 1966, 515–28.

_____, 'The date of Vegoia's prophecy', *JRS* 49 (1959) 41–5.

_____, 'Note sur la lettre Λ dans les inscriptions étrusques', in *Studi Banti*. Rome, 1965, 177–89.

_____, 'Recherches sur la fibule d'or inscrite de Chiusi: la plus ancienne mention épigraphique du nom des étrusques', *MEFRA* 83 (1971) 9–28.

_____, 'The Inscriptions of Pyrgi', *JRS* 56 (1966) 1–14.

Hoenigswald, H., review of A. J. Pfiffig, *Ein opfergelübde an die etruskische Minerva* (1968), *AJA* 75 (1971) 227–8.

Kaimio, J., 'The ousting of Etruscan by Latin in Etruria', in *Studies in the Romanization of Etruria. Acta Instituti Romani Finlandiae V.* Rome, 1972, 85–245.

Lambrechts, R., 'CII, SI 254. Nunc ubi sit comperi', in *Études Étrusco-Italiques*. Louvain, 1963, 101–9.

_____, *Les inscriptions avec le mot tular et les bornages étrusques*. Florence, 1970. Review by J. Heurgon, *Latomus* 31 (1972) 570–73.

Lejeune, M., 'Notes de linguistique italique, XIII: sur les adaptations de l'alphabet étrusque aux langues indo-européennes d'Italie', *Revue des Études Latines* 35 (1957) 88–105.

Maniet, A., 'Les correspondances lexicales de l'osque et du latin. Problème de méthode', in *Études Étrusco-Italiques*. Louvain, 1963, 131–43.

Mazzarino, S., 'Sociologia del mondo etrusco e problemi della tarda etruscità', *Historia* 6 (1957) 63–97, 98–112. On the survival of the Etruscan language in the Empire.

Meer, L. B. van der, '*Iecur Placentinum* and the Orientation of the Etruscan Haruspex', *BABesch* 54 (1979) 49–64.

Mingazzini, P., 'Sul fenomeno dell'aspirazione in alcune parole latine ed etrusche', *StEtr* 24 (1955–6) 343–9. On the Etruscan aspirates.

Olzscha, K., 'Einige etruskische Formen auf -cva und -chva', in *Gedenkschrift W. Brandenstein*. Innsbruck, 1968, 191–6.

Pallottino, M., 'Documenti per la storia della civiltà etrusca', in *Saggi di Antichità*, Vol. II, Rome, 1979, 475–863. Various articles, reprinted; some are listed separately in this bibliography.

_____, 'L'ermeneutica etrusca tra due documenti-chiave', *StEtr* 37 (1969) 79–91. Reprinted in *Saggi di Antichità*.

_____, 'Le iscrizioni etrusche', in *Atti dei Convegni Lincei. Le iscrizioni pre-latine in Italia, Roma 1977*, ed. G. Bonfante [1979] 39–44.

_____, 'La lingua degli Etruschi', *Popoli e civiltà dell'Italia antica* 6 (1978) 429–68.

_____, 'Nota preliminare sulla iscrizione del kantharos di bucchero del Metropolitan Museum di New York', *StEtr* 34 (1966) 403–6.

_____, 'Nota sui documenti epigrafici rinvenuti nel santuario', *Pyrgi. Scavi . . . 1959–1967, Notizie Scavi 1970. Supplemento* (1973) 730ff.

————, 'Il problema delle origini etrusche e la preminente incidenza del fatto linguistico nella sua discussione', in *Saggi di Antichità*, Rome, 1979, 191–7. Originally published 1977.

————, 'Rivista di epigrafia etrusca: Roma', *StEtr* 33 (1965) 505–7. On the earliest Etruscan inscription in Rome (*c*. 600 B.C.), discovered in 1963.

————, with the collaboration of G. Colonna, L. V. Borrelli and G. Garbini, 'Scavi nel santuario etrusco di Pyrgi', *ArchClass* 16 (1964) 49–117.

————, 'Spigolature etrusco-latine', in *Studi Funaioli*. Rome, 1955, 299–305. Reprinted in *Saggi di Antichità*. [Etr. *nunth(en)* and Lat. *nuntius*; *cerichu tesamsa* as equivalent of *faciendum curauit*.]

————, 'Sulla lettura e sul contenuto della grande iscrizione di Capua', *StEtr* 20 (1948–9) 159–96. Reprinted in *Saggi di Antichità*.

————, 'Sul valore e sulla trascrizione del *sigma* a quattro tratti', *StEtr* 35 (1967) 161–73.

————, 'Lo sviluppo socio-istituzionale di Roma arcaica. Alla luce di nuovi documenti epigrafici', *Studi Romani* 27 (1979) 11–12. Another archaic inscription from Rome.

Peruzzi, E., 'Appendix I. Mycenaeans and Etruscans', in his *Mycenaeans in Early Latium*. Rome, 1980, 137–49.

————, 'Romolo e le lettere greche', in his *Origini di Roma*. II. Bologna, 1973, 9–53.

Pfiffig, A. J., *StEtr* 35 (1967) 659–63. An inscription recently discovered at Tarquinia records the name of a man connected with Hannibal's campaign in the Second Punic War.

————, 'Zur Förderung nach moderner Sprachbetrachtung in der Etrus-kologie', *Die Sprache* 18 (1972) 163–87.

Poupé, J., 'Les aryballes de bucchero', in *Études Étrusco-Italiques*. Louvain, 1963, 227–60.

Prosdocimi, A. L., '*Vetusia* di Praeneste: etrusco o latino?', *StEtr* 47 (1979) 379–85.

REE, Rivista di Epigrafia Etrusca, continuing survey of inscriptions and readings, published in *Studi Etruschi*.

Rix, H., 'L'apporto dell'onomastica personale alla conoscenza della storia sociale', in M. Martelli and M. Cristofani, eds., *Caratteri dell'ellenismo nelle urne etrusche*. Florence, 1977, 64–73. Etruscan patronyms, ethnic names, and family names in the Hellenistic period.

————, 'Einige morphosyntaktische Übereinstimmungen zwischen Etrus-kisch und Lemnisch: die Datierungsformel', in *Gedenkschrift W.*

Brandenstein. Innsbruck, 1968, 213–22.

——, 'Zum Ursprung des römisch-mittelitalischen Gentilnamenssystems', in *Aufstieg und Niedergang der romischen Welt*, I, 2. Berlin and New York, 1972, 700–58.

Robb, K., 'Poetic sources of the Greek alphabet. Rhythm and abecedarium from Phoenician to Greek', in E. Havelock and J. P. Hershbell, eds., *Communication Arts in the Ancient World*. New York, 1978, 23–36.

Roncalli, F., '*Carbasinis uoluminibus implicati libri.* Osservazioni sul *liber linteus* di Zagabria', *JdI* 95 (1980) 227–64. A reconstruction of the original 'linen book' which was ripped up to make the bandages wrapped around the Zagreb mummy. Written in a north Etruscan city, *c.* 150–100 B.C., it was folded with 'accordion' pleats. Peculiarities of spelling, writing, etc. can be explained by its religious, ritual, archaistic character.

Simone, C. de, 'I morfemi etruschi -ce (-ke) e -che', *StEtr* 38 (1970) 115–39.

Torelli, M., 'Glosse etrusche: qualche problema di trasmissione', in *Mélanges Heurgon*. Rome, 1976, 1001–8. Their relation with the *disciplina etrusca*.

——, 'Il santuario greco di Gravisca', *Parola del Passato* 32 (1977) 398–458.

——, 'Scavi di Gravisca', *Parola del Passato* 26 (1971) 55ff. On a votive stone anchor from the Greek sanctuary of Gravisca, the port of Tarquinia; the 'Sostratos' recorded in the inscription may be the successful merchant mentioned by Herodotus.

INDEX TO SOURCES
(Sample inscriptions and texts)

CREDITS FOR ILLUSTRATIONS
(Not otherwise listed in text or captions)

1. Photo Sopr. Ant. Napoli, Caserta-Napoli. Courtesy Dr G. Buchner.
2. Cristofani, *Etruscans* 74.
4. Staccioli, fig. 12.
5. Pallottino, *Saggi di Antichità* (Rome 1979) 629–30, fig 40 (CIE).
10. Staccioli, fig. 3.
11. Sprenger-Bartoloni, *Etrusker* 11.
12. O. Montelius, *La civilisation primitive en Italie* (Stockholm 1895–1910) pls. 339–40.
14, 17. Drawings by A. Farkas.
15–16. Bonfante, *ED* figs. 68–9.
18. Dennis, *Cities and Cemeteries*, frontispiece.
19. Alinari, 2539.
20–4. *ES* 5.60; 112; 5.77; 238; 5.67.
25. Pfiffig, *Rel. Etr.* 162.
26–7. *ES* 83; 5.6.
28. Pfiffig, *Rel. Etr.* fig 10.
29. *ES* 5.127.
30–3. Pfiffig, *Rel Etr.*
34. Sopr. Ant. Etr., Florence.
35. Photo Vatican Mus. (copy).
36a, c. van der Meer, *BABesch* 54 (1979) 59–60
36b. Dumézil, *ARR* 653.
37a. Alinari, 2544; 37b. Staccioli, fig. 16.
38. Zagreb Nat. Mus.

INDEX